D1519911

HOMER
AND HIS INFLUENCE

BY
JOHN A. SCOTT
JOHN C. SHAFFER PROFESSOR OF GREEK
Northwestern University

MARSHALL JONES COMPANY
BOSTON · MASSACHUSETTS

THE PLIMPTON PRESS · NORWOOD · MASSACHUSETTS
PRINTED IN THE UNITED STATES OF AMERICA

Our Debt to Greece and Rome

EDITORS

GEORGE DEPUE HADZSITS, PH.D.
University of Pennsylvania

DAVID MOORE ROBINSON, PH.D., LL.D.
The Johns Hopkins University

CONTRIE ... TO THE "OUR DEBT TO
GREECE AND ROME FUND," WHOSE
GENEROSITY HAS MADE POSSIBLE
THE LIBRARY

Our Debt to Greece and Rome

Philadelphia

Dr. Astley P. C. Ashhurst
William L. Austin
John C. Bell
Henry H. Bonnell
Jasper Yeates Brinton
George Burnham, Jr.
John Cadwalader
Miss Clara Comegys
Miss Mary E. Converse
Arthur G. Dickson
William M. Elkins
H. H. Furness, Jr.
William P. Gest
John Gribbel
Samuel F. Houston
Charles Edward Ingersoll
John Story Jenks
Alba B. Johnson
Miss Nina Lea
Horatio G. Lloyd
George McFadden
Mrs. John Markoe
Jules E. Mastbaum
J. Vaughan Merrick
Effingham B. Morris
William R. Murphy
John S. Newbold
S. Davis Page (*memorial*)
Owen J. Roberts
Joseph G. Rosengarten
William C. Sproul
John B. Stetson, Jr.
Dr. J. William White
(*memorial*)
George D. Widener
Mrs. James D. Winsor
Owen Wister

The Philadelphia Society
for the Promotion of Liberal
Studies.

Boston

Oric Bates (*memorial*)
Frederick P. Fish
William Amory Gardner
Joseph Clark Hoppin

Chicago

Herbert W. Wolff

Cincinnati

Charles Phelps Taft

Cleveland

Samuel Mather

Detroit

John W. Anderson
Dexter M. Ferry, Jr.

Doylestown, Pennsylvania

"A Lover of Greece and
Rome"

New York

John Jay Chapman
Willard V. King
Thomas W. Lamont
Dwight W. Morrow
Mrs. D. W. Morrow
*Senatori Societatis Philoso-
phiae,* ΦBK, *gratias maximas
agimus*
Elihu Root
Mortimer L. Schiff
William Sloane
George W. Wickersham
And one contributor, who
has asked to have his name
withheld:
*Maecenas atavis edite regibus,
O et praesidium et dulce decus
meum.*

Washington

The Greek Embassy at
Washington, for the Greek
Government.

To

SAMUEL E. BASSETT

PROFESSOR OF GREEK IN THE UNIVERSITY
OF VERMONT, WHOSE VALUED FRIENDSHIP
INCREASES MY DEBT TO HOMER

1801.

CONTENTS

[vii]

HOMER
AND HIS INFLUENCE

HOMER
AND HIS INFLUENCE

I. HOMERIC POETRY AND ITS PRESERVATION

THE history of Greek literature begins with a double mystery, the mystery of the creation and the mystery of the preservation of the Homeric poems.

Homer is the sole literary representative of the heroic age, not a verse from earlier or from contemporary poets has survived. The names of these early poets have shared in the fate of their poetry, and there is little doubt that the songs of Musaeus, Linus, and Orpheus were never sung and that these names represent nothing more than fabulous poets.

Wonderful as is the fact that the *Iliad* and the *Odyssey*, with a combined length of almost twenty-eight thousand verses, should have survived the dark centuries which lay between Homer and the period of Athenian supremacy, it is hardly more wonderful than the second

[3]

fact that the Homeric poetry is the only poetry which survived essentially intact those other dark centuries which lay between Aristotle and the modern revival of learning.

Such famous names as Archilochus, Sappho, Alcaeus, and Simonides are hardly more than names, since they are known merely by the happy accident of chance quotation or torn papyri, while many of the successful dramatic competitors in the great days of the Athenian theater are hardly as much as names. Even Sophocles, the favorite in that great era, although he wrote more than one hundred plays, survives with but seven; the rest are lost or in fragments.

The Homer known to Plato, Aristotle, and the illustrious scholars of Alexandria is practically the same Homer which is known to us; a thing which is true of no other poet of early or of classical Greece.

All of the Greek poets whose poetry has escaped oblivion owe that escape to isolated passages or to fortuitous references in late writers, or to few and incomplete manuscripts, all except Homer. The complete manuscripts of Homer are almost without number, so many are they that the Oxford Edition of Homer is based on nearly one-hundred-and-fifty manuscripts, most of which are good, so good that almost any two or three would suffice to establish the Homeric text.[1] All these manuscripts are reinforced by constantly increasing masses of papyri and by a practically unlimited number of quotations in the works of Greek and Latin authors.

Homer is sometimes referred to as the poet of other early epic poems as well as of the *Iliad* and the *Odyssey*, but he is never definitely thus mentioned by writers of the best period. Aristotle and the scholars of Alexandria always drew a distinction between the poetry of Homer and the other poems of the early epic cycle.

Late writers frequently quote as from Homer verses and phrases which are not to be found in the *Iliad* and the *Odyssey*, hence has grown up the assumption that these verses belonged to Homeric poems which are now lost. Homer by his very eminence became an easy source for all kinds of poetic quotations, some of which are luckily to be found in other early poems of known authors: Macrobius, *Saturnalia*, V. 16.6 says that Homer stuffed his poetry with proverbs, then he quotes six ex-

[5]

amples of this stuffing, two of which are to be found not in Homer but in the *Works and Days* of Hesiod. Even so learned a writer as the Emperor Julian quoted as from Homer a verse which belongs to this same *Works and Days*.[2]

The best early authorities discuss the fact that Homer never tells except by allusions the events which began and closed the Trojan War, and their reasoning is of such a nature as to prove that there was then no well-established belief in the Homeric authorship of the poems of the *Cycle*.

The people of Colophon erected a statue to Homer and engraved thereon: " Thou didst bring forth with thy divine soul two daughters, two poems in honor of heroes, the one telling of the return of Odysseus, the other of the war at Ilium." [3]

The references to Homer as the author of epic poems other than the *Iliad* and the *Odyssey* are so vague, so dependent on difficult interpretation of doubtful passages, and so at variance with the clear affirmations of the most reliable ancient authorities that it is hardly possible for Homer's name to have been connected with these epics until in comparatively late times.

Most Homeric scholars disagree with me in this and think the *Cycle* was regarded as Homeric in the Early Classical period.

Antiquity assigned to the youth of Homer a comic or satirical poem, the *Margites*. The hero of this poem was a stupid youth who "knew many things, and knew them all badly." This poem was probably a bit of farce and may well have been a youthful caricature drawn by the same hand which later sketched a Thersites and a Polyphemus. We cannot with the scanty fragments as evidence challenge the judgment of Aristotle who unhesitatingly assigned the *Margites* to Homer.

The *Batrachomyomachia, Battle of the Frogs and the Mice,* is often mentioned as Homeric and it is sometimes printed along with the other poetry of Homer. This poem is a parody on the *Iliad,* a parody in which frogs and mice arm, speak, and fight in the grand manner of the Homeric heroes. It is an exceedingly clever poem, but the language shows evidence of being far later than the language of Homer, while there are allusions to events which could not be earlier than the sixth century. This poem is Homeric only in so far as it is a parody on Homer and written

[7]

in the dialect of the early epic. No competent authority has ever assigned the *Batrachomyomachia* to Homer.

There is also a group of thirty-four hymns, the so-called *Homeric Hymns*, written in the dialect and meter of Homer. These hymns appear to have been used to introduce the recitation of other longer poems and to have been composed in honor of the divinity or hero at whose festival the bard was singing. Some of these hymns might have been the only song then sung, but the shortest could have been nothing more than an introduction to a longer poem. Thucydides quotes one of these hymns as if it were composed by Homer, but the language is clearly much later than that of the *Iliad* and the *Odyssey*, and although we for convenience, as well as Thucydides, speak of these hymns as Homeric, we cannot regard them as the work of Homer.

A few minor epigrams, riddles, and the like have found a place in the complete works of Homer, but they are universally regarded as late and spurious.

From earliest times the reputation of Homer has depended on but two poems, the *Iliad* and the *Odyssey*, and these two poems in essentially their present form. We thus have all the evidence in forming our estimate of his ability that was known to the ancients, except the lost poetry of the epic cycle. However, we have the decided advantage of the new sciences of archaeology and of comparative linguistics; also we can understand Homer better by reason of the rediscovery of early Cretan, Egyptian, and oriental civilizations.

The excavations made in Troy, Mycenae, Crete, and elsewhere have shown something of the civilization and the legends inherited by the age of Homer, and we are thus assisted in visualizing the life he described and in estimating the sort of material with which the poet worked. By the help of comparative linguistics we are able to restore a lost consonant and to explain many seeming metrical irregularities which were the despair of ancient scholars, while the recently won knowledge of oriental civilizations has solved the difficult problem of writing in Homer and has shown the strong bonds binding early Aegean and Asiatic life and traditions.[4]

A large part of the contributions to Homeric scholarship during the last century and a quarter has been concerned with the problem of the origin of these poems, that is, whether the *Iliad* and the *Odyssey* are each a unit and both the work of the same genius or whether they are the product of many bards working through several generations.

The controversy is still unsettled, but there has been a great change in recent years and most scholars now agree that these poems picture essentially the same civilization, the same general theology, and that they represent the same stage of linguistic and literary development.

Those who believe in one Homer and those who believe in many are alike forced to rely on something akin to a miracle, and the point at issue is simply this: Is it more reasonable to suppose that there was one supreme genius who created two such similar and stupendous works of art, or that there were many such poets, each master of the same grand style, and all having the same poetic purposes and all in control of the same poetic powers?

Greece never had the slightest doubt that these two poems were the creation of a single man, and it seems best for us in company with all antiquity to believe that early Hellas had one poet capable of creating these two poems, rather than that she had several men gifted with any such powers, and then forgot them.

Not all parts of Homeric poetry are of the same merit, and it is easy to pick out scenes in which there seems little energy and inspiration, but no three parts of these poems show such diversities as are shown by *The Two Gentlemen of Verona, Hamlet,* and *A Midsummer-Night's Dream.*

The observation has been made by competent critics that Homer has more sustained grandeur and less variation than Shakespeare.

It is probable that Homer had no rivals in his own age, and also that he had no predecessors who could have begun, as he had no followers who could have completed his poems. Such writers as Dante, Cervantes, Shakespeare, and Milton may have had associates, but the works on which their fame is based were not done in collaboration.

The French *Chansons de Geste,* with their numberless songs around a common heroic theme, seem to have all the necessary conditions for a great epic poem, all but the great epic poet himself. They probably represent much the same stage of poetry as would have been represented by early Greece in its songs

and epic cycle, if Homer had not been. The
Ballads of Spain have been called " Iliads without Homer." It is just the one fact of Homer
that gives glory to heroic Greece.[5]

In all the great ages of literature the outstanding achievements have been the work of
single individuals and not of schools, groups,
or masses of inspired and creative singers.

The plan and the workmanship of the *Iliad*
and the *Odyssey* show that they were each
conceived as a whole and were not the result
of gradual or fortuitous additions. It is also
evident that they have never been subjected
to any serious or lasting revision and that no
one ever had the power and the will to improve
or to rewrite them.[6]

Some simple proofs that Homer has never
been subjected to serious revision are these:
Pylaemenes was slain in the action of the fifth
book of the *Iliad*, but he is alive to mourn the
death of a son in the thirteenth book. This
contradiction regarding a subordinate character would have seemed a trifle to the original
poet, but would have been a serious matter to
revisers, as it has been to all the critics, and
had it been in the power of the revisers they
would certainly have removed that contradic-

tion. The change of a single word in the first passage or the addition of a negative in the second would have been all that was needed, but that slight revision was not made.

Odysseus in the presence of the Phaeacians boasted that he was the best archer of all the Greeks who fought at Troy; yet when the contest in archery was held in the Games of the *Iliad*, Odysseus did not even compete, although he had been a contestant in several events. Homer did not care about this discrepancy, as the hero was simply engaging in some epic boasting, but nervous revisers, without the fires of creative impulse, would have removed the difficulty by quietly substituting Odysseus for the winning archer in the story of the *Iliad*.

A like explanation must be given for the failure of the poet to mention at the death of Hector the fact that he was protected by the armor of Achilles, his slayer; also for the silence of the same poet regarding the treachery of Pandarus when he fell at the hands of Diomede.

Such passages as these in which the hearer is left to fill out the gaps and to draw his own inferences, as well as many other unrevised inconsistencies, " Homeric nods," furnish abundant evidence for the belief that the poetry of Homer has not been seriously revised or interpolated.

This evidence is confirmed by the well-known conservatism of the Greeks, a conservatism which banished Onomacritus, a favorite of Pisistratus, for adding a verse to the poetry of the mythical Musaeus, and which fined Lycon, a friend of Alexander, the huge sum of ten talents for interpolating a single verse in an Attic comedy.

The Homeric poems could hardly have escaped linguistic weathering or modernization, also certain stock verses might have been added, others dropped or transposed, but with these minor exceptions it is probable that no change has been made in the text of Homer since its creation. It must be remembered that the language of Homer is unlike the dialect of any of the historical peoples of Greece and that the most remote Hellenic lands and cities all quoted him in his own speech, they did not transfer him to their own.

These two poems are much longer than the 27,853 verses might imply, and the frequent assertion that Spenser's *Faerie Queene* with its

35,000 verses is as long as the *Iliad,* the *Odyssey,* and the *Aeneid* combined rests on a wrong inference. The verse used by Spenser has, except the last verse of the stanza, but ten syllables, while the shortest possible Homeric verse has twelve, the longest seventeen, and the average is between fifteen and sixteen. One hundred verses in Homer have as many syllables as one-hundred-fifty-five in Spenser; therefore the combined length of the *Iliad* and the *Odyssey* is much greater than that of the *Faerie Queene.* Bryant's translation of the *Iliad* into English pentapody has just under 20,000 verses.

In all these Homeric verses there is not a single gap, not one incomplete line, not a verse too long or too short, but all alike have the finished mark of the same artist.

II. HOMER AND TRADITIONS
IN HOMER

THOUGHTFUL as tradition has been of the poems, the poet himself it has almost neglected. His name is found in no early writings and on no old inscriptions, and he is first mentioned as Homer in the writings of Xenophanes of Colophon, that is near the end of the sixth century B.C., while the words *Iliad* and *Odyssey* first appear in the history of Herodotus, that is in the second half of the following century.

Although the name of Homer was so late in appearing in extant literature, no writer of early Greece threw any suspicion on the existence of a real poet or upon that poet as the creator of both the *Iliad* and the *Odyssey*. All the early Greeks took him as much for granted and as familiar as their own mountains and streams, so that they seemed to feel no mystery concerning him and rarely made a conjecture regarding his age, his nativity, or his genius.

We have no definite facts upon which to base a life of Homer but must rely on vague inferences drawn from the poems themselves, and, as these poems never contain the name Homer and seemingly never refer to the place of his birth, his age, or his contemporaries, even these vague inferences are largely a matter of conjecture. It seems strange that Homer did not try to win favor for himself by adding to his poems the praise of some living potentate, a trait so pronounced in the poetry of Virgil, Horace, and Tennyson.

The absence of definite local descriptions regarding the place of his nativity and the great reputation of his poems led many cities to claim him as their own. Among the various cities claiming this honor Smyrna's claim has been most widely accepted, since the radiation of the knowledge of his poems seems to have had its center in that city.

Homer was also called Melesigenes, a name evidently derived from the river Meles, a river of Smyrna, on whose banks he is said to have been born.

Poets often refer to him as Maeonides, a word beautifully adapted for poetry. The origin of this name is doubtful; it is sometimes derived from Maeonia, an early name for Lydia, but it is more likely a true patronymic, as his father was supposed to be Maeon, who was said to have been both the uncle and the father of the poet.

Next to Smyrna the neighboring island of Chios has the best claim for the birthplace of the poet, and, even if it be denied this honor, it is generally believed to have been the site of much of his labors.

The date of Homer's birth is most uncertain, since the first known attempt to fix it was made by Herodotus who argued that Homer had lived about four-hundred years before his own time, that is, he assigned Homer to about 850 B.C.

The recent discoveries in pre-Homeric civilizations in and near the Aegean basin, as well as the results of linguistic investigations, strengthen the ancient belief that Homer was a native of Smyrna, also that he lived not far from the beginning of the ninth century. There is great disagreement among scholars in both of these matters, but while it is possible that Homer may have lived as early as the eleventh century it is hardly possible for him to have been later than the ninth.

[18]

Although archaeology in recent years has done much to illuminate Homeric poetry, the poet himself is as remote and elusive as ever.

Many attempts have been made to explain the name Homer as that of some trait or character and not the proper name of an individual, asserting that it was a common noun and meant a " blind man," a " hostage," or a " joiner." The last assumption was made in the attempt to prove that Homer was not regarded as a creative poet, but was simply the " joiner " who arranged into one the poetry already existing. Now it is asserted by those who wish to give a Babylonian origin to the *Iliad* and the *Odyssey* that this is not a Greek word at all, but a true Babylonian common noun meaning a person who sings.[7] It is the beauty of all such theories that the derivation of the name Homer so often supplies just the needed support. The name of the poet is so evasive that this very fact may prove that it is a true proper name, since most Greek proper names do not easily reveal their origin.

The extreme skepticism which marked all phases of Homeric criticism during the last century is now changing to the belief that Homer is the name of a real person, that the

Iliad is the poetic description of a real war fought in a real place, and that this war was a struggle between the Greeks and the Trojans.[8] The story of the *Odyssey* is so interwoven with the mythical and the impossible that its historical residuum must be almost negligible.

Back of all early Greek literature there lay an indistinct mass of tradition to which poets went for plots and suggestions, and which they interpreted with the greatest freedom. Paris in Homer seems to have had no other wife than Helen and his amours seem the escapade of impetuous youth; yet there was another tradition that he had deserted an affectionate and noble wife, Oenone. There is not a hint of this earlier marriage in Homer, since this would have utterly ruined that gentility and courtesy which dignified the portrait of Helen. She could not have seemed so attractive and so humble if there had been a wronged and a jealous wife in the background. Hesiod, the poet nearest in time to Homer, says that Helen bore to Menelaus a daughter, Hermione, and a son, Nicostratus; while Homer distinctly stresses the fact that Helen bore but one child, Hermione.

[20]

Even the parentage of so important a goddess as Aphrodite was a matter of contradictory traditions; in Homer she was the daughter of Dione, while in Hesiod she was denied both father and mother and was represented as springing from the sea-foam which gathered around the mutilated parts of Uranus as these parts floated on the surface of the waters.

When a Greek artist chose for his theme some scene from Homer he rarely made an attempt to illustrate the text of the poet, but he changed the setting almost at will, *e.g.* Agamemnon in the story of the *Iliad* sent two heralds to bring Briseis from the presence of Achilles, a scene which is pictured on a familiar vase, but the artist of the vase did not choose to represent Briseis as moving along with two heralds, hence he substituted Agamemnon for one of them, thus absolutely violating the plot of the poem.[9] This was of little moment to him, as he was chiefly interested in the beauty and harmony of his picture.

Such a thing as orthodoxy in Greek tradition was practically unknown and each poet or artist varied the myths which he handled almost at will. This tradition was the storehouse to which epic, lyric, and dramatic poets alike went for their heroes and their background.

Homer, Pindar, and Sophocles went to this store-house for hints with which to stage or to embellish their poetry, but not for the poetry itself. Pindar took these hints and composed lyric poetry, Sophocles took them and wrote dramatic poetry, and Homer in an earlier age took these same hints and turned them into the *Iliad* and the *Odyssey*. It was due to the accident of time and changing customs that Homer created epic rather than lyric or dramatic poetry out of this traditional material. The "Homeric Question" owes its being to the fact that the epic has been assumed to be a form of literature absolutely unlike anything we know from historical Greece; while the truth is, Homer differs from the other Greeks only in time and in genius.

The varying treatment of the same subject by the different dramatists shows how little poets strove to reproduce an existing and familiar tradition. Milton also took a traditional theme in *Paradise Lost,* yet he hardly owes two-hundred verses to that tradition, and he based one entire book on the brief passage in the Bible which begins with the words " and there was war in heaven."

Where the imagination of the poet had such free play it is clearly impossible to reconstruct from the poems themselves the traditions from which he drew.

Homer plunges at once into the midst of his story, as if he assumed that the plot and the actors were known to his hearers, but he then so fills in the details and adorns the matter that we are as fully informed by him as if he had assumed our entire ignorance of the subject.

The poet rarely tells in details matters concerning which we are warranted in assuming an existing tradition. He tells us that the Greeks were held at Troy by the anger of Athena, but he does not explain the origin of that anger. He tells us that Ajax, the son of Oileus, was most hateful to Athena, but the reason is not given. He hints at, (without describing), the death of Antilochus and of the greater Ajax.

These known silences regarding traditional matters, and the simple fact that the poet never describes, but always assumes as known, implements, customs, and landscapes with which his hearers were familiar, make it highly probable that he is not repeating an old and familiar tale but that he is himself creating new traditions.

The details and the manner of the telling make it more than possible that the wrath of Achilles and the return of Odysseus never had received extended poetic expression until Homer made them the theme of his poems.

Although the poetry of Homer is the oldest poetry of Europe, it is not primitive poetry, for the poet is not striving after an unreached mastery in meter, ideas, or language. There are no experiments, but absolute control of one of the most difficult of meters, of the most complex syntax, and of the largest vocabulary used by any poet of Greece. The distinction generally drawn between natural epic and literary or conscious epic, with Homer as the type of the natural and Milton of the literary epic, is utterly false. Homer is no less literary than Milton and no definition of the essence of epic poetry can be framed which does not include them both.

Homer was a conscious artist who knew the worth of his own work, and who constantly referred to the immortality of glory which

[24]

would be the portion of the actors in his own imperishable songs. It seems the arrogance of genius that he could trust his own enduring renown to poems which do not even contain his name.

Somehow Homer was able to reach poetic effects which seem easy and natural but which have been reached by none besides. Virgil was a great and conscious artist who also wrote dactyls, but many of his dactyls seem slow and labored when compared with Homer's, and Bréal has made the shrewd observation that it takes less effort to read fifty verses of the *Iliad* than twenty of the *Aeneid*.[10]

Aristotle, the best possible judge of Greek poetry, said that the *Iliad* and the *Odyssey* surpass all other poems in diction as well as in thought. Primitive poets may have the thoughts, but noble diction belongs only to advanced art.

Homer is so hidden by his own creations that we cannot get a glimpse of him, except as these creations reveal his greatness. We can only surmise his ideas as we find them revealed by the deeds or the words of the actors in the poems. The only consistent tradition concerning Homer was the tradition of his blindness, but the poems show such delicate and varied powers of observation that his blindness has generally been considered impossible. However there is another side to this matter and the words of Helen Keller show that the poetry of Homer can arouse the enthusiasm of the blind: "It was the *Iliad* that made Greece my paradise. I cannot measure the enjoyment of this splendid epic. When I read the finest passages I am conscious of a soul-sense that lifts me above the narrow, cramping circumstances of my life. My physical limitations are forgotten — my world lies upward, the length and the breadth and the sweep of the heavens are mine!"[11] A poet who could so appeal to the emotions of the blind may himself have been blind, since the possibilities of creation and of enjoyment are subject to the same limitations, or as it has been better said by Goethe,

Du gleichst dem Geist den du begreifst,
(*You are like the spirit which you comprehend.*)

It is hard to draw any conclusions concerning the purposes of the poet from his own works, but we are sure that the oft-repeated assertion that " in Homer we have the com-

[26]

plete picture of a civilization " is entirely false,
as is the other statement that " Homer wove
so many histories together as contained the
whole learning of his time." One needs but
to think of the matters Homer does not mention in order to grasp how much he has
neglected. Everything connected directly with
the " wrath " is fully set forth, no knowledge
is there presumed, but it is only by inference
that we can connect its story with the events
which preceded or followed, or can form an
opinion regarding the poet's theology or his
civilization.

Did the poet know of the sacrifice of Iphi-
genia at Aulis, of the festering foot of Phil-
octetes, of the manner of the death of the
Dioscuri, and of a hundred other important
matters connected with the siege of Troy or
with the actors of the *Iliad?* He probably
did, but as they were not involved in the
" wrath," he passed them in silence.

Helen came on the scene prominently in the
Iliad and was one of the mourners at the bier
of Hector, where she uttered dark forebodings
of an unhappy future. Paris was still her
husband, but when she reappears in the
Odyssey there is no narrative of her subse-

quent fate at Troy, and there is not an inkling
of what became of Paris, since even his name
is unmentioned in the second poem.

No actor human or divine is so much in
evidence and so powerful in both poems as
Athena, but the poet makes no reference to
the manner of her birth, while Hesiod tells
the story of her springing from the head of
Zeus as if it were an old and familiar tale;
neither does Homer name the mother of Helen,
except indirectly, since the only reference
to Leda is as the mother of Castor and
Pollux.

When we are left in darkness concerning
such prominent characters as Athena, Paris,
and Helen we can realize how scanty is the
light thrown on minor events and actors.

Homer had no ulterior motive in his poetry
and he presented no system of learning, of
morals, of theology, of government, or any
outline of history. The *Iliad* has an historical
background and an actual local setting, but
these are only incidental, a stage on which the
great tragedy of love, sorrow, passion, and
death is acted. The appreciation of Homer does
not depend on a knowledge of either history
or geography, for the qualities which make the

Iliad great are not of the Trojan war, but of all time.

There are no nature forces, no nature myths hidden beneath the characters of Helen, Odysseus, Hector, and Achilles, but they meant to Homer and to his hearers exactly what they mean to unsophisticated men today. The Greek character shows an astounding permanency and we know that when in the days of Sophocles the Athenians watched on the stage the miseries of the house of Atreus they were looking at real human sorrows, no nature forces in disguise. We are justified in supposing a like feeling in Homer and also in his hearers.

Homer has long been praised as a moral teacher, but it is hard to find any such purpose in his poetry. The fury felt by Athena and Hera for the Trojans was not from a sense of wrong but because of their own wounded pride, and that fury is never assigned to the adultery of Paris; Zeus could not fathom it and repeatedly but in vain urged them to remember the sacrifice and piety of the Trojan leaders. The poet never mentioned the death of Paris; a sure proof that he had no intention of showing that the wrath of the gods followed to the end the betrayer of his host. There seems no moral reason for the anger of Poseidon which so ruthlessly followed Odysseus because he escaped from the cave of Polyphemus in the only manner escape was possible.

It is hard to picture an all-powerful and all-good God as reigning in a world in which there is evil, a difficulty which was met by Hebrew and Christian theology by assigning all the evil to the Devil. Homer with no conception of a Devil that is only evil, held the gods responsible for both the good and the bad. Homer's gods would have presented a far holier aspect, if there had been in the poet's mind a Devil who was solely responsible for the immoral and ignoble acts of men.

The Homeric gods seem due to the sense for moderation and for beauty which inhered in the Greek people rather than to any theological reforms of the poet himself. He was so indifferent to giving a digest of theology that in the *Odyssey* the divine action is practically limited to Athena, although Zeus is all-powerful in the background, while Poseidon's anger thwarts the efforts of the hero for a season. The only appearance of Ares,

[30]

Apollo, Aphrodite, and Hephaestus in the
Odyssey is in the song of Demodocus; a song
that is hardly didactic or theological in its
tendency.

The Iliad *and the* Odyssey *are simply
imaginative, ecstatic, poetic creations, unhampered by any ulterior moral, historical, theological, or philosophical purposes.*

III. TRANSLATIONS OF HOMER

THE poetry of Homer is so melodious in meter, vocabulary, and inflection that it is impossible to give even a faintly adequate idea of its beauty by means of paraphrase or translation. A paraphrase into English prose of Milton's *Lycidas* or of an ode of Keats would destroy all the charm, but would have the advantage of the same language and essentially the same vocabulary, while the paraphrase of Homer, even into Greek, shows the amazing elevation of Homeric meter and Homeric language.

The prose rendering of the *Iliad* published as an addition to the scholia has but a single word unchanged in the paraphrase of the first verse of the *Iliad,* and that one word, the word for goddess, is not the usual prose form but is highly poetic. In English we can scarcely produce more than this prose paraphrase, while the music and the magic inhere only in the original words of the poet.

Many phrases which cannot be brought into English without becoming the flattest prose or the worst metrical drivel are expressed in the original by words of melody and of majesty, *e.g.* Homer refers to kine as " eilipodas helikas bous," a peculiarly charming group of sounds, yet the English thereof " cattle with crumpled horns and shambling gait " is common prose which cannot be turned into melodious English by any genius of poetry.

It is hard now to grasp the reasons for the great repute gained by Chapman's Homer, as it is so unlike and so much more difficult than the original, and I have often been obliged to turn to the Greek in order to find the meaning Chapman intended to convey. A reading of this famous translation gives hardly an inkling of the style or excellencies of Homer. In book VI of the *Iliad,* verse 401, Hector's infant son is said to be " like a beautiful star," just three simple Homeric words in the Greek, but in Chapman we have:

> *Like a heavenly sign,*
> *Compact of many golden stars, the princely child*
> *did shine.*

When Andromache told Hector of the death of her father, she said, "About his tomb the mountain nymphs, daughters of aegis-bearing

Zeus, caused elms to grow." These few and plain words appear in Chapman thus:

> The Oreades, that are the high descent
> Of Aegis-bearing Jupiter, another of their own
> Did add to it, and set it round with elms; by which
>   is shown
> In theirs, the barrenness of death; yet might it
>   serve beside
> To shelter the sad monument from all the ruffinous
>   pride
> Of storms and tempests, used to hurt things of that
>   noble kind.

Again in that same speech Andromache said, " Mother ruled as queen under woody Placus until Artemis delighting in arrows slew her in the halls of my father." This appears in Chapman:

> And she in sylvan Hypoplace, Cilicia ruled again,
> But soon was overruled by death; Diana's chaste
>   disdain
> Gave her a lance, and took her life.

The pun on the words " ruled " and " over-ruled " has no warrant in the original, while " Diana's chaste disdain gave her a lance," seems most remote from the dignity and simplicity of Homer.

When Chapman had finished his task of translating Homer he exclaimed, " The work that I was born to do is done! "

This translation gave Chapman a place among the great poets of his great age, Swinburne addressed Chapman as "High priest of Homer! ", and in the face of Keats' testimony we cannot doubt the thrill this translation brought to a true judge of poetry; yet one who has both Homer and Chapman before him must regret that Keats could not have written another sonnet upon reading Homer in Homer's own language.

Chapman's translation was long an English classic, an honor that was also won by Pope. While Chapman's Homer has steadily declined in popular favor, Pope's is still widely read.

There is a swing and a movement in many parts of Pope which might rival Homer himself. The first eight verses of Pope's *Iliad* are as follows:

Achilles' wrath, to Greece the direful spring
Of woes unnumber'd, heav'nly goddess, sing!
That wrath which hurl'd to Pluto's gloomy reign
The souls of mighty chiefs untimely slain;
Whose limbs unburied on the naked shore,
Devouring dogs and hungry vultures tore;

Since great Achilles and Atrides strove,
Such was the sov'reign doom, and such the will of
   Jove.

This is great poetry, but it is not Homeric, even if it does vaguely reproduce the opening lines. Hades becomes " Pluto's gloomy reign," while the simple words, "He gave them as a spoil for dogs and for all birds of prey," become:

   Whose limbs unburied on the naked shore,
   Devouring dogs and hungry vultures tore.

" Unburied on the naked shore," " devouring," and " hungry " are entirely due to Pope. These few verses are a good illustration of the liberties Pope took with the original, so that one must smile to see Sir John Lubbock gravely quoting Pope to illustrate Homeric customs of marriage, when the thing quoted is solely due to Pope and not to be found in Homer.[12]

The greatness of these opening verses has given this translation a reputation it scarcely deserves, for it is in just such passages as these that Pope is at his best. He has missed "the grand style of Homer " utterly and in scenes of simple narrative he is too ornate, often bombastic and absurd. The plain words of Homer, " Lambs have horns at their birth " become in Pope:

> And two fair crescents of translucent horn
> The brows of all their young increase adorn,

and the phrase " horns wrapped with gold " becomes:

> Whose budding honours ductile gold adorns.

Not only are such commonplace facts foreign to the genius of Pope, but he is even worse in such noble scenes as the parting of Hector and Andromache, as he then felt it necessary to improve on Homer. This scene begins with the verse: " But he found not his faultless wife within," which Pope thus improves:

> But he found not whom his soul desired,
> Whose virtue charm'd him as her beauty fired.

All through this noble scene Pope stresses the physical attractions of Andromache, so that Homer's beautiful words, " Thus speaking he placed his son in the arms of his mother," become the tawdry:

> He spoke, and fondly gazing on her charms
> Restor'd the pleasing burden to her arms.

[37]

Homer never hints at the physical beauty but glorifies only the spirit of Andromache, and this is vulgarized by Pope.

Pope's *Homer* is one of the most illustrious books of English authorship. Young in his *Night Thoughts* paid its author this great tribute:

Dark, though not blind, like thee, Maeonides!
Or Milton, thee! Ah could I reach your strain,
Or his who made Maeonides our own,
Man too he sung.

Coleridge referred to " That astounding product of matchless talent and ingenuity, Pope's *Iliad*." [13]

This great and lasting reputation is deserved, but Pope never caught the style or the spirit of Homer.

The translation by Cowper is far superior to either Chapman's or Pope's as an interpretation of the poet, but it lacks a certain fire and swing essential to winning great poetic renown. Along with Cowper's should be placed the careful and successful translation by Bryant.

A poetic translation of the *Iliad* has been made by the Earl of Derby, which is accurate, dignified, and poetic. This seems to me to reproduce Homer more nearly than any other English verse translation, but even these verses in the heroic measure of Milton bear little resemblance to the majestic and flowing hexameters of the original.

Most attempts to render Homer in English dactyls have ended in failure, for the simple reason that our language has few dactylic words or forms and it has too many mono-syllables, while dactyls need a language abounding in sonorous and polysyllabic words. Longfellow achieved a large measure of success in his *Evangeline,* but such verses as:

Loud laugh their hearts with joy and weep with pain as they hear him,
White as the snow were his locks and his cheeks were as brown as the oak leaves,

are dactylic by sufferance only and have little to connect them with the majestic dactyls of Homer.

A worthy translation in dactylic hexameters by H. B. Cotterill has been highly praised to me by Doctor Walter Leaf.

The most satisfactory translations are those in prose, of which there are several of high

merit.   The best known are the *Iliad* by Lang,
Leaf, and Myers, the *Odyssey* by Butcher and
Lang, and the *Odyssey* by Palmer.   A recent
translation of the *Odyssey* by A. T. Murray,
published in the *Loeb Classical Library*, is
especially good.

The prose of these latest translators comes
nearer to the original than any poetic version,
yet no more reproduces Homer than a char-
coal sketch can reveal the beauties of a Titian,
but it does give a fairly accurate impression of
what the poet said.

IV. THE ILIAD

THE first word of the *Iliad* is "Wrath" which reveals at once the kernel of the poem, since the *Iliad* does not depend on the fate of Achilles, but solely on his wrath. There are no unanswered questions concerning this wrath, its origin, its course, or its results; but the death of Achilles, the return of Helen, the end of the war seem hardly nearer than when the poem began. The historical element in the *Iliad* is thus but slight, even if it does concern an actual war.

The speeches of the quarrel scene and of the embassy, the pleadings of Thetis with Zeus, the parting of Hector from Andromache, the making of the shield, the games, the father begging for the delivery of the corpse of his son are all poetic creations, unhampered by time or place.

Recent excavations made at Troy and geographical surveys in the Troad are of great value and prove that the poet chose a real city and an actual landscape for his setting, also that he was describing a civilization that had once existed, but, even granting all this, Homer has none the less given to " airy nothing a local habitation and a name."

A real Mt. Ida there must have been, but the scene thereon between Zeus and Hera is still mythical; genuine is the wall of Troy, but Helen's appearance at its summit and Hector's parting from Andromache are merely the creation of the poet's fancy.

Into the story of Achilles' anger the poet has woven most of the great human emotions and has endowed all his actors with an individuality that has never been surpassed. It is easier to enter into familiar companionship with the great Homeric creations than with Miltiades, Themistocles, Thucydides, or with most of the historical characters of Greece. We know Nestor better than we know even so famous a man as Pericles, in spite of Thucydides, Plutarch, and the comic poets.

The *Iliad* introduced to literature such outstanding figures as Agamemnon, Achilles, Hector, Paris, Priam, Diomede, Nestor, Odysseus, Helen, Hecuba, and Andromache. Each appears as a distinct personality and has ever since preserved the Homeric features.

A discussion of the plot and the great scenes of the *Iliad* would far transgress the limits set for this book, yet the poet's ability to set forth striking ideas in a few words may be illustrated by a series of brief quotations and running comments.

Nestor, a speaker whose talking pleased others and himself, is described as "a speaker from whose lips speech sweeter than honey flows." The conservative Odysseus put into a single sentence the slogan of autocracy: "A government by the many is not a good thing. Let there be one ruler, one king to whom Zeus has given dominion," and Helen's description of Agamemnon as "both a good king and a mighty warrior" has been the ideal of aspiring princes.

When Agamemnon saw that Menelaus had been shot, in violation of the truce, he exclaimed: "Not in vain are the sacred oaths, the blood of lambs, and solemn compacts, for if Zeus does not show his power at first, he will in the end punish mightily the guilty with utter destruction."

Strife is described as "small at first but at last it strides with its feet on earth and head in heaven," an image which Virgil repeats but

HOMER AND HIS INFLUENCE

applies to Rumor (*Fama*). Nestor grieved
that although he had years and experience he
was without youth and vigor, then comforts
himself by saying: "The gods have never yet
given all things at the same time to any man."
This has been repeated by Virgil in his famous
phrase:

Non omnia possumus omnes.

Axylus is described as "a man who lived in
a house by the side of the road and gave hos-
pitality to all." This evidence of a sense for
social service has been the subject of many an
address or essay.

The words of Glaucus, "As is the race of
leaves, so is the generation of men, the wind
casts some leaves to the ground, others the
flourishing forest brings forth when spring has
come, so is the generation of men, one is born
and another passes away." This has the honor
of being the first quotation made by any
ancient writer where the nativity of the poet
of the *Iliad* was given. Simonides quotes it as
by the man of Chios. Shelley was much im-
pressed by these lines and incorporated them
in one of his youthful poems.

This same Glaucus, in his enthusiasm at

finding an ancestral friend in Diomede, exchanged his own armor of gold for Diomede's armor of bronze, the proverbial example of those who in a moment of excitement throw away on trifles their most precious possessions; and this is the Greek equivalent of "selling one's birthright for a mess of pottage."

Zeus boasted that he was so strong that he could draw up earth and sea, then suspend them in air, bound with a golden chain to a spur of Olympus. This "golden chain" or *aurea catena* was a prominent element in later philosophical theories of the universe.

Odysseus tried to arouse Achilles by saying: "There is no means for finding a cure when once the evil is done," but Achilles replied: "Cattle and sheep may be won back, tripods and horses be seized, but you cannot recover the human life that has once departed from the body."

Hector's reply to Polydamas, who had tried to check him in his victorious career because the omens of birds were unfavorable, is absolutely modern and is often regarded as the finest expression of patriotism ever spoken. "You bid me put my trust in broad-winged birds, but I refuse to follow them, I care not

whether they move to left or right. One omen
alone is best, to fight for native land." Professor Gildersleeve pronounced this last verse
"the world's greatest verse of poetry." It is
translated by Pope with a superb couplet:

Without a sign his sword the brave man draws,
And asks no omen but his country's cause.

This however misses the simple dignity of the
original, since Homer used but six words. It
seems to me that Chapman missed the tone
absolutely in his: "One augury is given to
order all men best of all: Fight for thy coun-
trie's right." The Earl of Derby's rendering
is nearly perfect:

The best of omens is our country's cause.

On another occasion Hector inspired his
men with the words: "It is glorious to die
fighting for one's native land," and this has
been repeated by Horace in the verse:

Dulce et decorum est pro patria mori,

a motto which has been a favorite inscription
on military monuments.

During the struggle for the body of Patro-

clus deep night spread over the field, when
Ajax in anguish prayed that Zeus might slay
him, if he only gave him light. This has been
adapted by Longfellow:

> The prayer of Ajax was for light;
> Through all that dark and desperate fight,
> The blackness of that noonday night,
> He asked but for the return of sight,
>   To see his foeman's face.[14]

When the warriors were preparing for battle
down in the plain, the old men too feeble to
fight sat on the walls " chirping like grass-
hoppers," as they discussed the merits of the
different chieftains, or sat in silence while
Helen pointed out and named for them Agamemnon, Odysseus, Ajax, and Idomeneus.
Longfellow with wonderful aptness drew on
this scene for his poem, *Morituri Salutamus,*
delivered on the occasion of the fiftieth anni-
versary of his graduation from college:

> As ancient Priam at the Scaean gate
> Sat on the walls of Troy in regal state
> With the old men, too old or weak to fight,
> Chirping like grasshoppers in their delight
> To see the embattled hosts, with spear and shield,
> Of Trojans and Achaians in the field;

[47]

So from the snowy summits of our years
We see you in the plain, as each appears,
And question of you; asking, 'Who is he
That towers above the others? Which may be
Atreides, Menelaus, Odysseus,
Ajax the great, or bold Idomeneus?'

When the corpse of Patroclus came back to his tent Briseis uttered a dirge of bitter sorrow, grieving in his death, and all the women joined therein: "apparently weeping for Patroclus, but in truth each wept for her own sorrows."

When a laugh was forced from the angry Hera it is said that "She laughed with her lips but there was no joy in her face."

Andromache described the cup of charity which is doled out to orphans, as: "a drink which moistens the lips but does not reach to the palate."

When Hector challenged the best of the Greeks to meet him in single combat: "They all remained silent, ashamed to refuse but afraid to accept."

The aim of education was to make one "a speaker of words and a doer of deeds."

When Achilles mourned for Patroclus he said: "I shall never forget him, so long as I share the lot of the living, and if they forget the dead in Hades, even there will I remember my beloved companion."

Bellerophon carried to Lycia a secret order for his own death, a thing which suggested to Young in his *Night Thoughts:*

> He *whose blind thought futurity denies,*
> U*nconscious bears, Bellerophon! like thee*
> Hi*s own indictment: he condemns himself.*

Zeus uttered the amazingly frank statement: "There is nothing more wretched than man, nothing of all the things which breathe and move on the face of the earth." This sentiment is very like the words of Achilles: "The gods have decreed that wretched mortals should live in sorrow, while they themselves are free from cares."

The following verses are much quoted and self-explanatory:

Potent is the combined strength even of frail men.
Sleep which is the brother of death.
The purposes of great men are subject to change.
Whoever obeys the gods, him they especially hear.

When two go together, one thinks before the other.
Good is the advice of a companion.

[49]

War is impartial and slays the slayer.

Zeus does not bring to pass all the purposes of men.

Even a wood-chopper accomplishes more by skill
than by strength.

A fool can understand, when the thing is done.

Whatever word you utter, just such a word you will
be obliged to hear.

The actors of the *Iliad,* excepting gods and
priests, are all warriors or their dependents
and the poem is drawn with a military setting,
but the real greatness of that poem is in the
portrayal of powerful human emotions rather
than in military exploits.

No blood is shed in the first three books of
the *Iliad* and there is no fighting in the last
two. Strange as it may seem only a minor
part of the poem is given to actual warfare,
while most of the great scenes are without
fighting.

Even those books which are most martial,
such as the fifth, have long stretches in which
no blood is shed.

The world has always been interested in
wars and in warriors, so that many of the
most famous names of history belong to military heroes. Homer wisely chose this absorb-

ing theme as the background of his poem, but it is little more than the background, the setting. So great was his genius that he drew scenes of battle with such power and painted war with such faithfulness that a Napoleon was convinced that the *Iliad* was the work of an expert military tactician,[15] but the poet's heart was elsewhere and it was far different qualities which he honored.

Patroclus was much the greatest Greek warrior to be slain in the action of the *Iliad*. When his body was in danger of falling into the hands of the foe, Menelaus urged the Greeks to the rescue with these words: " Let each one now remember the gentleness of poor Patroclus, for he knew how to be gentle to all." The fact that the companion of this great warrior should recall the gentleness and not the prowess of the fallen leader shows the sentiments of the poet. Homer was able so to stress the kindlier elements in the character of Hector as to win for him the appearance of greatness in spite of his repeated military failures.

Of all the Homeric similes but five are taken from warfare, and of the 665 tropes no more than fifteen are military.[16]

There were other sources of fame than war, since the assembly was called "man-ennobling," and the council is referred to as "the place where men become very conspicuous." In the *Odyssey* a good speaker is said to be "preëminent among assembled men, and when he moves throughout the city the people gaze at him, as if he were a god." How different all this from the feelings of a real war-poet, Tyrtaeus, who said: "A man who possesses every excellence is nothing, if he be not mighty in war! "

The Homeric warriors were all men of might, but still they were men. Achilles could be wounded and he had no abnormal traits or powers, such as mark the heroes of most sagas. In the Indian epics the heroes uproot mountains and slay their foes by the thousands. The bow of Rama must be carried by five thousand men. In the Irish tales the hero has seven pupils in each eye, and in his anger flames stream from his mouth while a jet of blood higher than the mast of a ship shoots up from the top of his head. In these Irish epics men are slain by thousands through the might of a single arm.[17] The exploits of Achilles, though great, are within the limits of the possible and they seem almost tame in comparison with the thrilling adventures of some of the decorated heroes of The World War.

V. THE ODYSSEY

THE CHARACTERS of the *Iliad* are drawn to an heroic scale and with an heroic poise, Thersites excepted, but in the *Odyssey* even the hero himself during most of the poem is in the guise of a suppliant or of a beggar, while the other actors are slaves, revelers, or men of rank, and kings who do not show their crowns and their scepters.

Odysseus in the *Iliad* was one of the eight or ten outstanding leaders, but he was clearly not in training for the great part he was to take in the companion poem. When Hector challenged the best of the Greeks to meet him in single combat they decided to select his antagonist by lot, and as the lot was cast they all prayed that "Ajax, Agamemnon, or Diomede might be chosen," but no one wanted Odysseus to have this dangerous honor. In the contest for the prize in archery he did not compete, yet in the *Odyssey* he boasted that he easily excelled all those at Troy who handled the bow.

[54]

The hero of the *Odyssey* is a re-creation of the Odysseus of the *Iliad,* the same in gifts, but greatly exalted. Then, too, the wife, Penelope, is never named in the earlier epic. The poet did not introduce the hero in person until in the fifth book of the *Odyssey,* since the impression must be created that he is of such importance that his fate is eagerly discussed not only in Ithaca, Pylos, and Sparta, but among the assembled gods of Olympus as well.

The action of the *Iliad,* as far as the human actors are concerned, is confined to the limited area of the Troad, while the hero of the *Odyssey* moves from Troy to the land of the Cicones, then throughout the length of the Aegean, thence out into fairyland and back to Ithaca. Telemachus journeyed to Pylos and to Sparta, Nestor told of his return voyage from Troy, while Menelaus recounted his adventures in Egypt and his visit to many lands, even to Phoenicia and Libya.

The greatest single difference between the *Iliad* and the *Odyssey* is the difference of setting, for the action of the *Iliad* is confined to a single small district, the action of the *Odyssey* moves without restraint over limitless regions, going even into fairyland and to Hades.

The plot of the *Iliad* is loosely joined, so loosely that there are many books which contribute little or nothing towards the advancement of the story. The sixth, ninth, and twenty-third books are three of the greatest of the poem, yet had they been lost from the manuscripts and never been quoted, one could hardly have suspected their existence. This does not mean that they were additions by later poets, since if most of the soliloquies of *Hamlet* had been lost it would have been hard to detect the gaps. The important eleventh book is only vaguely connected with the books immediately preceding.

In the *Odyssey* the structure is just the reverse, for in it there is such a mutual interchange of cause and effect that each book can be understood only in the light of earlier books. Athena in the first book came from Olympus to arouse Telemachus to go in search of his father; in the second an assembly is called and this search is announced as well as prepared. In this the poet had a double purpose, he showed us the wife, the son, the suitors, the faithful Euryclia, and the conditions in Ithaca, and we are made to realize the great importance of the hero himself.

In the next two books the young man made the trip to Pylos and to Sparta as ordered and planned, and we learn the heroic stature of Odysseus from his own companions and associates at Troy.

Just such an introduction as is given in these books is needed to make the hearer feel that the Odysseus he had known in the *Iliad* is fitted for the great part he was destined to assume. Had the *Odyssey* opened at book five the poet could not have created the impression that the Odysseus he had left at the games of the *Iliad* had become sufficiently important to warrant his holding the center of the stage, and holding it throughout the entire poem. This journey of Telemachus had another purpose and that was the furnishing of an opportunity for the immature youth to develop under new influences into the hero he proved to be in the great struggle with the suitors.

The long story of Odysseus' wanderings could have found no ready and eager audience without the songs of Demodocus and the exploits at the games. Even the mysterious movements through fairyland have a necessary sequence, since the crews who manned the twelve ships with which he sailed from Troy were far too numerous to be entertained by Circe, hence the destruction of the eleven ships at the hands of the Laestrygones must precede the story of the sojourn in the Aeaean isle. Even one shipload was too many men for the seven years with Calypso, hence the slaughter of the cattle of the sun and the shipwreck, but the adventures with Charybdis and Scylla demanded a ship and its crew, hence they came earlier than the storm which brought the loss of all his companions.

It is doubtful if the skill with which the poet of the *Odyssey* weaves the individual strands of poetry into a great epic plot has ever been equalled. This is the second great difference between the two poems, since the *Iliad* is a succession of loosely joined scenes, a series of pearls strung on the thread of the anger of Achilles, and so strung that many of them might have been removed without detection, while the *Odyssey* is a complicated chain of poetry, a cable in which each strand strengthens and is strengthened by all the rest.

Professor Sheppard wisely suggests that the *Iliad* is to be compared to a pattern or a complicated drawing, where the seemingly isolated books really serve as decorative panels, and that each individual scene somehow adds to the beauty and the completeness of the whole.[18]

Not a single hero of the *Iliad* who appears in the first book is on the scene at the close, even the setting is changed from the shore and the camp of the Greeks to the city and the assembly of the Trojans; while the *Odyssey* which has shifted so much and has moved to so many and such remote regions closes in Ithaca, on the estate of Odysseus, and among the actors with which the poem began; even Athena who set in motion the forces which started the poem and brought the hero to his home is the last to act and to speak.

In setting and in structure these two poems are quite different, however similar they may be in style, in meter, and in language. The *Odyssey* never repeats or imitates the *Iliad* but always assumes a knowledge of the events of that earlier poem as a background.

The ancients regarded the *Odyssey* as a later poem than the *Iliad*, but the evidence is surprisingly slight. The words of Proteus to Menelaus, "and you were present at the battle," were intended as a reason for not repeating things told in the *Iliad* and warrant the inference that the narratives of that poem were already known.

The *Odyssey* constantly assumes a knowledge of the story of the *Iliad*, while the *Iliad* never makes any assumption of a knowledge of the *Odyssey*.

The *Iliad* apparently took over but little foreign material; perhaps the Catalogue of the Ships, and the story of Meleager, as told by Phoenix, were such foreign material. The *Odyssey* unites the adventures of the hero with a mass of stories and myths, some of which may be traced to other lands and to remote antiquity. Sir Arthur Evans thinks he has found in the ruins of early Crete representations of the myth of Scylla,[19] while tales resembling the story of the Cyclops have been found in many lands. However, the wanderings of Odysseus have been so cleverly united with the blinding of Polyphemus that we can scarcely imagine an *Odyssey* without that adventure.

The Lotus-Eaters, Aeolus, Circe, Calypso, Scylla, and Charybdis may all be older than Homer, but they are so fitted into the story, so interwoven with the exploits of Odysseus that they have the dignity and the freshness of new creations.

Fairyland seems real in Homer, and the descriptions of the abode of Calypso and of the house and the gardens of the Phaeacians are the most definite and elaborate in either poem. The poet does not assume that they are known to the hearers, hence the very fullness of the description may prove that they are due entirely to his fancy.

Verses from the *Odyssey* that have passed into general literature are the following:

All men feel their need of gods. (A favorite verse of Melanchthon.)

Fear not in your heart, for a bold man is better in every undertaking.

Nothing is more pleasing than one's native land.

Eager to pile Ossa on Olympus, and Pelion on Ossa.

On the one side Scylla, on the other Charybdis.

All forms of death are bitter to man, but the worst death of all is to die from hunger.

One man finds delight in one thing, another in something else.

It is an equal evil to press a guest to leave when he desires to remain, or to force him to stay

when he wants to depart. One should enter-
tain the guest while he is present, then let
him go when he wishes to depart.

Pope's translation of one of these verses:

Welcome the coming, speed the parting guest

is deservedly famous, but is supposed to be
due to his collaborator, Broome.

A man finds joy in evils, when they are past.
The very presence of the weapon tempts to violence.
God brings like unto like.
In adversity men quickly grow old.
To confer a favor is better far than to do a wrong.
It is a sin against the gods to boast over a fallen
    foe.
Hard it is to refuse a gift.
To spend one's time in talking trifles is evil.
Things in moderation are better.
A man has no greater glory so long as he lives than
    the athletic prizes he wins with his hands and
    his feet.

This sentence is peculiarly Hellenic and seems
also much like the faith of the college student.
Homer could not have better expressed the
present enthusiasm for athletics.

Evil deeds do not prosper.
Worthless are the pledges of worthless men.

When Odysseus and his men were in the presence of great danger he encouraged them by reminding them of the trials through which they had successfully passed, then added:

Some time, no doubt, you will fondly recall this
     danger too.

Virgil brilliantly took over this idea in these words: *Forsan et haec olim meminisse juvabit.*

Too much sleep is a burden.

Schliemann had this last sentence put as a motto over the door of his bed-chamber.

Odysseus came to the hut of the swineherd in the guise of an infirm beggar and told his host that once he had been a man of might, but as he realized that his present condition was not in harmony with that boasted greatness, he added:

By looking at the stubble you can certainly com-
     prehend (that is, how great the harvest must
     have been).

[63]

The gods have never yet shown themselves to all men.

It is a terrible thing to shed royal blood.

This was a favorite motto with partisans of Charles the First.

Stern are the rebukes of princes.

Evil shepherds destroy the flocks.

A man loses half of his manhood when he becomes a slave.

Shyness ill becomes a man in want.

Men are easily generous with another's wealth.

It is better to die than to live a failure.

A drunkard finds misery for himself first of all.

May health be thine and great joy, also may the gods grant thee prosperity.

The *Odyssey* is the tale of an island-ruler who returned after long years to his distracted realm, slew the conspirators against his home and his power, and by re-establishing his authority brought peace to his kingdom.

A modern poet would have made the re-union of the husband and wife the climax of the poem, but the love motif is secondary in Homer, and the goal is not reached until it is evident that the death of the suitors is to

[64]

remain unavenged, until the strife has been settled and the hero firmly fixed on the throne he inherited from his fathers. The present close of the *Odyssey* is thus a necessity by the very conception of the poem. The *Odyssey* is not, as already said, a series of scenes but a closely connected plot, fully thought out from the beginning.

Even the many fairy tales told at the Phaeacians' banquet must have been in the first formulation of the plot, since the loss of all the companions is a necessary part of the story; yet these companions were lost in fairyland and it was in fairyland that Poseidon found the reason for his anger.

When Odysseus left Troy he had twelve ships and hardly less than six-hundred followers, but when he reached home his ships were wrecked and he was all alone. It is most unlikely that any explanation for this change was ever put in verse except in the present narrative of our *Odyssey*.

The *Iliad* has more fire, more passion than the *Odyssey,* hence is to be regarded as the greater poem, and it has been more often quoted, but the handling of the material, the technique, of the *Odyssey* is incomparably superior. The *Odyssey* is the work of Homer when the poetic fires have somewhat cooled, but when he had thoroughly mastered the minutest details of epic composition.

There are three compositional defects in the *Iliad,* as follows: first, the elimination of the hero from the story for long continuous stretches; Achilles is not even named in the third book; second, the action is overcrowded on two of the important days, since all the events from the beginning of the second book until near the close of the seventh are supposed to come between dawn and dusk of a single day; also the fighting which began at the opening of book eleven does not abate until near the middle of book eighteen; third, there is no necessary sequence or causation for many of the events of the poem, that is, some books are so loosely connected with the narrative that they scarcely advance the story.

All these defects are completely mastered by the poet in the *Odyssey,* as the hero is never forgotten and is hardly less prominent in the books from which he is absent than in those in which he appears; the events are so well distributed that no day is crowded with excess action; and, finally, the poem is an organic whole, each part contributing to the plot, each scene depending on what has preceded and influencing that which is to follow.

These points of superiority in the *Odyssey* seem due to experience and they seem to prove that this poem is the work of the poet's artistic maturity, although that maturity marks a certain decline in poetic ecstasy; thus supporting the ancient belief that the *Iliad* was the work of Homer's younger years, the *Odyssey* of his ripe and advancing age.

VI. THE REACH OF HIS GENIUS

HOMER shows his greatness alike in the immense reach of his genius and in the execution of the most minute details and in the ability sympathetically to portray the most varied characters. His Zeus is worthy to be the king of the gods, so that poets as well as artists have made him their ideal of that exalted divinity; yet his Zeus is no better done than the swineherd, the old nurse, or the innocent girl, Nausicaa.

With a single act, speech, phrase, or description the poet is able so to fix personal traits or attributes that his characters take on an individuality distinct from all the rest. Stentor is given but two lines, yet his name has become an adjective of almost universal use, even appearing as a scientific term of definite application.

Thersites appears but once and makes but a single speech; yet he has ever since been the representative of his class, as clear and distinct as if he had been a leading actor. When Emerson wrote: "Some figure goes by which

Thersites too can love and admire," no one can
doubt his meaning.   Goethe refers to this one
speech by Thersites as:
*das herrlichste Original einer sansculottischen
Demagogenrede.*

Helen, Andromache, Hecuba, and Penelope
were all wives and mothers, but the poet has so
pictured them that each represents something
quite apart from the other three.   Nausicaa,
the young princess of the Phaeacians, appears
in but two books, yet she is so charming and
so human, so like none but herself that she has
lived in literature as the perfect example of
gracious maidenhood.   Goethe planned a
drama with her as a leading character, but
abandoned the idea, since he did not wish to
compete with the original.

Homer could create a Zeus fit to rule over
gods and men, he could set forth the passions
of an Achilles and put in his mouth speeches
of royal rage and dignity, then he could just
as lovingly bring in the old slave Dolius and
could put on his lips the tenderest of all
greeting; for when Dolius knew that Odysseus
had indeed returned, he kissed his hand at the
wrist (a wonderful little touch!) and said:

" May health be thine and great joy, may the gods also grant thee prosperity." The same genius could with equal fidelity linger lovingly by the side of the poor old dog, Argos, that cast out with fleas and filth died of a broken heart, broken for joy at sight of his kind and affectionate master who had left him twenty years before. The poet does not think it unworthy of the hero of so many struggles to add: " At sight of him Odysseus turned aside his face and wiped away a tear."

It is the self-consciousness of his own powers which makes a poet presume to compose speeches for Achilles, Odysseus, Zeus, and Athena; but the real test of this self-confidence is found when he undertakes to compose the song sung by the Sirens. Circe had warned Odysseus that he must hasten by the Sirens, since they charm all men who come near them; then she added that no one who had once heard their melodious strains could bring himself to leave them, while all about were the bones of men who had died as they tried to listen. There was only one means of safety and that was to fill the ears of his companions with wax while he himself was to be securely bound to the support of the mast.

[70]

Odysseus, as ordered, stopped the ears of the crew with wax, had himself securely bound hand and foot and then started to sail past the Sirens, but when their song was heard he determined to delay and to listen, even if this meant destruction, but his companions, who could not hear, bound him in yet stronger fetters, carried him out of the reach of the voice of the Sirens, and thus saved the ship and the crew.

It must have been an entrancing song which could induce a cool and crafty Odysseus, in spite of definite warning, to throw away his hopes of Ithaca and of life, just to listen for a moment to its strains. Homer does not shrink, he gives the song.

This song is of unusually rich melody even for Homer, a melody which inheres in the original Greek and is lost in the translation, so that it is possible to show but dimly its beauties: " Come hither, illustrious Odysseus, great glory of the Achaeans, and moor your ship, for no one has ever passed us by until he has heard the mellifluous song from our lips. When he has once heard he goes on with great joy and with increased knowledge, since we know all things such as the Argives and the Trojans

[71]

brought about through the will of the gods, and we know all things which have ever taken place on the face of the fruitful earth."

In this song there is no appeal to the sensual, but only to his pride and to his eagerness for knowledge. It was the proffer of knowledge which tempted Eve in the Garden of Eden, and Odysseus would have fallen, as Eve fell, if he had not been saved by the wax in the ears of his companions, for they were out of the reach of temptation. Homer agrees with the Biblical narrative in believing that the desire for knowledge is the strongest of all human appeals.

Although Homer dared to put in words the song of the Sirens, he did not dare to describe the beauty of Helen, yet he was able to give a wonderful impression of that beauty by showing the effect it had on others, and those others were not passionate and susceptible youths but the old men of Troy. As these old men, too feeble to fight, yet full of bitterness at the misery Helen had brought to them, sat on the walls of their city they saw her approaching, and as they looked on her face they forgot their resentment and could only say: " It is no wonder that Trojans and Greeks have suffered

[72]

long for such a woman, since her face is as the face of an immortal god." When men in their plight could not think of censure because of the beauty of such a woman, she must have been surpassingly beautiful.

Omitting such minor characters as Dolon, Calchas, Theoclymenus, Pisistratus, and others of that secondary prominence, of whom there are at least a score who act and speak, also omitting all the gods and omitting all the shades encountered in Hades and all the characters of Fairyland, we find that Homer has created or made use of about forty leading actors. Each of these forty speaks and acts with an independent and definite person-ality, so that it is possible to form a picture and to write a character sketch of him. Compare this with the almost total absence of individualism in the characters of most of the twelve disciples named in the New Testament!

Spiess in his *Menschenart* [20] *und Heldentum* has drawn pen-portraits of twenty-seven actors of the *Iliad* alone. All of these actors, found in both poems, are portrayed with such power, such distinctness, that it is impossible to say that Homer excels in presenting any one class

[73]

of people. Of these forty leading characters, but four, Nestor, Menelaus, Odysseus, and Helen, take part in both poems.

Homer's willingness to create different types of characters seems endless, and the genius which created a bluff and dense soldier such as an Ajax tarried for a moment to sketch the delicate figure of a Nausicaa, merely that Odysseus might have a guide to the palace of the Phaeacians. The poet could have economized by permitting the hero to observe the palace from some eminence and then by allowing Athena to direct his going; a thing the goddess really did in the end.

The crossing out of a few verses would completely detach Nausicaa from the story of the *Odyssey*. Nausicaa furnishes abundant proof that we are not dealing with uninspired compilers or careful revisers, but with the lavish extravagance of thriftless genius.

No one of all these actors in Homer represents a type, but all are human beings with the limitations and the contradictions of real people.

Homer has over two-hundred complete similes and also many simple comparisons, such as " Apollo came like the night," or

"Thetis arose like a mist." These similes are so vivid and so easily understood that they have furnished a poetic storehouse for the most varied writers; even a book so remote as Fielding's *Tom Jones* abounds with similes in the Homeric manner.

The religious element in Homer is so subordinated to poetic ends that it is impossible to frame an Homeric theology, yet the gods control all; men may delay but cannot thwart their purposes. The will of Zeus is always decisive but he was under the constant influence of Athena, who in both poems accomplishes her aims by winning the approval of her all-powerful father.

Homer's gods seem only remotely connected with righteousness, and the prayers always assume that the one praying has put the gods under some obligation and thus the prayer is a demand for the repayment of a favor. The first prayer of the *Iliad:* "O Apollo, if I have ever roofed for thee a pleasing temple, or have burned for thee the fat thighs of bullocks or of goats, then grant me this request," shows the worshipper's attitude.

All Homeric prayers are practical and are appeals for victory, vengeance, or prosperity, but there is no fervent seeking for a pure heart or for personal righteousness.

The gods are represented as all-knowing, all-powerful, and everywhere-present, but, even so, they can be deceived and their plans frustrated in contradiction of their omniscience and omnipotence; while in the first book of the *Iliad* the action was delayed because the gods had gone to a long revel with the Ethiopians and could not be consulted,—a flat denial of their omnipresence.

The evident immorality and helplessness of the Homeric gods early caused heart-burnings in the devout admirers of the poet and they tried to explain away their misgivings by the assumption that these gods were largely natural forces and that they were to be understood only as allegories. This one example will explain the method: Hephaestus is said by Homer to have been hurled down from heaven and only after lying helpless for a long time to have been restored to life, but he never completely recovered from the effects of this fall and he continued to hobble with a distorted leg. This unnatural cruelty of a father to his faithful son is thus explained: "Hephaestus is an allegory for the two forms of fire, the heavenly and the earthly fire. The fire in the heaven is perfect and needs no fuel, the fire that has come down to earth is imperfect and must be fed. The earthly fire is fed or supported by wood, and as lame men walk with wooden canes, so the fire that feeds on wood is said to be supported by something like a cane, hence is itself called lame."

In Homer there are no military or priestly classes. When Menelaus, Nestor, Odysseus, and the rest returned to their homes they doffed their armor and took up work of much the same nature as that done by the common people. Among the progressive states of Greece, soldiers and priests never thwarted the search for truth and the efforts to establish liberty under law; the thing that more than all else separated the thinking of the Greeks from their Egyptian or Asiatic neighbors. All this is in Homer, but it is hard to believe that he single-handed created that tolerant atmosphere to which the world owes the great intellectual achievements of Hellas.

The Homeric gods have long lost their influence in the realm of theology but they still hold their place in the mechanism of poetry, even in the imagination of a public

[77]

but dimly acquainted with antiquity. The gods of Norse or of Hindu mythology have not supplanted the gods of Homer in the poetic sphere, and his muse is still the patron of song.

When Hamlet pictured his father as having:

The front of Jove himself,
An eye like Mars to threaten and command,
A station like the herald Mercury,

he is using Homeric mythology and is paralleling, if not imitating, the description of Agamemnon as given in the *Iliad:*

His eye, and lofty brow the counterpart
Of Jove, the lord of thunder, in his girth
Another Mars, with Neptune's ample chest.

In the *Tempest,* Shakespeare introduces Iris, Ceres, Juno, and the Nymphs as speaking in Homeric character, and Iris says of Aphrodite:

I met her deity cutting
The clouds towards Paphos, . . . in vain
Mars' hot minion has returned again.

This is drawn from the song of Demodocus in which Aphrodite after her frustrated tryst with Ares sped back to Paphos, the seat of her favorite shrine.

The use of Homeric mythology is all-pervasive and in all grades of literature, from the highest flights of Shakespeare and Milton to the last jokes in the daily papers and the excited descriptions of the latest prize-fight.

Closely akin to mythology is the long list of famous men and women who have passed from the verses of Homer into the common language of the race and who stand for something akin to human types: Hecuba, the broken-hearted mother, Priam, the faithful and aged father, Nestor, the wise but garrulous old man, Paris, the fop and the coward, Hector, the noble husband and the self-devoted prince. The contrast between the things which these brothers represent is well shown in the familiar verses of Longfellow:

> Better like Hector in the field to die
> Than like a perfumed Paris turn and fly.

Hector was not only the devoted warrior but he was a brother who felt deeply the shame brought on the family and city by Paris, and, because of the indignation over that shame, he soundly berated him, hence this side of his nature has given the words " to hector " and "hectoring," words found in the writings of a man as remote from the stream of the classics as John Bunyan.

Achilles is still the type of the outspoken and fearless youth who preferred an early death to seeming dishonor; also the other side is shown in the phrase, "sulking Achilles," or even when he is not named, in the expression, "sulking in his tent," with a reference to his anger.

Ajax represents the big and powerful fighter who relies on his brute strength and sweats under a seven-fold shield. Shakespeare refers to him as "beef-witted Ajax." In modern industry machines and equipments of great power are often named after him, and the city of Chicago alone has sixteen factories which make various Ajax tools or devices.

Teucer, the clever archer, Patroclus, the faithful companion, constantly appear in modern literature, while the very name of Mentor, the guide of Telemachus, has come to mean guide, counsellor, and friend.

In addition to these prominent actors there are the mythical figures of Circe and Circe's wand (so characteristic is this wand that it is still used by magicians and conjurers of every sort), Calypso, Charybdis, Acheron, Aeolus, Aeëtes, the Argo, Ariadne, the Amazons, the Aethiopians, Ate, Amphitrite, Alcmena, Alcestis, Halcyone, Amphiaraus, Amphitryon, Asclepius, Assaracus, Atlas, Bellerophon, Boötes, Briareus, Ganymede, the Giants, Daedalus, Dardanus, Deucalion, Dionysus, Enyalius, Hesperus, Eumelus, Eurystheus, Eos, Themis, Thetis, Thyestes, Jason, Idas, Hippotades, Iris, Cadmus, Cassandra, Castor and Pollux, the Centaurs, the Cimmerians, the Cyclops, Laomedon, Marpessa, Memnon, Minos, Niobe, Paeeon, Panope, Oedipus, Pirithous, Pelops, Proteus, the Sirens, Semele, the Gorgon, Jocasta, Sisyphus, Scylla, Tantalus, Tithonus, the Titans, Hyperion, Chiron, Chimaera, the Pygmies, the Lotus-Eaters, the Symplegades, Thamyris, Medea, Orion, and Hercules.

All these are referred to under attributes with which they have ever since been joined. It may be that these later traditions were created out of inferences drawn from Homer; but it seems more probable that the poet was referring to familiar tales, tales which somehow survived without being incorporated in the poetry of Homer.

To these should be added such words as nectar and ambrosia, the drink and food of the gods; nepenthe, a drug or magic something which deadened the sense of grief or pain; moly, an herb capable of withstanding the powers of sorcery; ichor, a fluid flowing in the veins of the gods; a sardonic smile, and Homeric laughter, also rosy-fingered dawn; even the word Iliad has passed into a figure of speech in such a phrase as " an Iliad of woes," and Odyssey in such an expression as " an Odyssey of adventures."

How important the words of this above list are in modern literature will be shown by one of the lesser and more obscure of the number, Proteus.

VII. PROTEUS IN ENGLISH LITERATURE

MENELAUS was unable to get away from the island of Pharos and in his extremity was met by Eidothea who urged him to form an ambush and seize her father, Proteus, who had the gift of prophecy and who, if firmly seized, would direct Menelaus in methods of escape and would tell him also how things at home had fared during his long absence. She slew and flayed four seals which belonged to the flock of Proteus, then she concealed Menelaus and three companions under these skins of the seals and told them to await the approach of the aged sea-divinity and seer, Proteus. About noon the sea-god came out of the deep and, having numbered his seals and found that none was missing, he lay down near them and went to sleep. Menelaus and his companions threw off the skins of the seals and tried to seize the aged Proteus, " But the old man forgot not his crafty art and became first of all a bearded lion, next he took the form of a serpent, a panther, and a huge boar, and then he changed into the likeness of running water, after which he became a tree with towering branches, but all this time we held on with determined purpose."

At last when Proteus saw that his wiles were in vain and that his captors would not let him go, he assumed his wonted form, became again an old man of the sea and told Menelaus how he could resume his journey from the island, also revealed the fate of many of the companions he had left at Troy, and ended by assuring him of his blessed immortality in the fields of Elysium which he was to enjoy with his restored and untarnished Helen. "Thus having spoken he sank under the billowy waves of the sea," and he did not reappear, at least in the poetry of Homer.

This is the Homeric story of Proteus and most literary references depend on it:

Spenser: *The Faerie Queene:*

He then devisde himselfe how to disguise;
For by his mighty science he could take
As many formes and shapes in seeming wise,
As ever Proteus to himselfe could make:
Sometime a fowle, sometime a fish in lake,

[84]

Now like a foxe, now like a dragon fell. (I, 2, 10.)
And, for his more assuraunce, she inquir'd
One day of Proteus by his mighty spell
(For Proteus was with prophecy inspir'd)
Her deare sonnes destiny to her to tell. (III, 4, 25.)

Then like a Faerie knight himselfe he drest;
For every shape on him he could endew:
Then like a king he was to her exprest,
And offred kingdoms unto her in vew
To be his Leman and his Lady trew
But when all this he nothing saw prevaile,
With harder meanes he cast her to subdew,
And with sharpe threates her often did assayle;
So thinking for to make her stubborne corage quayle.

To dreadfull shapes he did himselfe transforme:
Now like a Gyaunt; now like to a feend;
Then like a Centaure; then like to a storme
Raging within the waves. (III, 8, 40 and 41.)

Shakespeare:

I'll play the orator as well as Nestor,
Deceive more slyly than Ulysses could,
I can add colours to the cameleon,
Change shapes with Proteus, for advantages.

The words of Richard: *Henry VI*, Part III, III, 2.

Sometime a horse I'll be, sometime a hound,
A hog, a headless bear, sometime a fire;
And neigh, and bark, and grunt, and roar, and
      burn,
Like horse, hound, hog, bear, fire, at every turn.

The words of Puck: *A Midsummer-Night's*
      Dream, III, 1.

Proteus is the name of the treacherous and
fickle lover in the *Two Gentlemen of Verona*.

Milton:

In vain, though by their powerful art they bind
Volatile Hermes, and call up unbound
In various shapes old Proteus from the sea,
Drained through a limbec to his native form.
                    Paradise Lost, III, 602.

The song in *Comus* 867 ff. abounds in
Homeric allusions and in it Proteus is called
"the Carpathian Wizard," a typical example
of Milton's display of great erudition.

Dryden: *Hind And Panther*, III, 818:
      O *Proteus conscience, never to be tied!*

Pope: *The Dunciad*, I, 37 ff:
Hence bards, like Proteus long in vain tied down,
Escape in monsters, and amaze the town.

[86]

The Dunciad, II, 129 ff:
> So *Proteus, hunted in a nobler shape,*
> Became, *when seized, a puppy or an ape.*

Satire, The First Epistle of The First Book
of Horace, 151:
Did *ever Proteus, Merlin, any witch*
Transform *themselves so strangely as the Rich?*

Thomas Gray: *The Characters of The Christ-
Cross Row*, 43:
> *Proteus-like, all tricks, all shapes can show.*

Shelley: *Prometheus Unbound*, III, 2, 24:
Blue *Proteus and his humid nymphs shall mark*
The *shadow of fair ships;*

Ibidem, III, 3, 65 ff:
Give *her that curved shell, which Proteus old*
Made *Asia's nuptial boon, breathing within it*
A *voice to be accomplished.*

The Triumph of Life, 271 ff:
If *Bacon's eagle spirit had not leapt*
Like *lightning out of darkness — he compelled*
The *Proteus shape of Nature as it slept,*
To *wake, and lead him to the caves that held*
The *treasure of the secrets of its reign.*

Coleridge: *Lines To An Autumnal Evening,*
      45 ff:

Or mine the power of Proteus, changeful God!
A flower entangled Arbour I would seem
To shield my love from Noontide's sultry beam:
Or bloom a Myrtle, from whose odorous boughs
My Love might weave gay garlands for her
      brows.
When Twilight stole across the fading vale,
To fan my Love I'd be the Evening Gale;
Mourn in the soft folds of her swelling vest,
And flutter my faint pinions on her breast!
On Seraph wing I'd float a dream by night,
To soothe my love with shadows of delight: —
Or soar aloft to be the Spangled Skies,
And gaze upon her with a thousand eyes!

In his *Biographia Literaria,* II, 20, he refers to
Shakespeare thus: " Shakespeare passes into
all forms of human character and passion, a
Proteus of the fire and the flood, he becomes
all things, yet for ever remains himself."

Wordsworth: *Miscellaneous Sonnets,* XXXIII:

The world is too much with us: . . .
. . . Great God! I'd rather be
A Pagan suckled in a creed outworn:
So might I, standing on this pleasant lea,

[88]

Have glimpses that would make me less forlorn;
Have sight of Proteus rising from the sea.

To the Clouds, 72 ff:

                              Moon and stars
Keep their most solemn vigils when the Clouds
Watch also, shifting peaceably their place
Like bands of ministering spirits, or when they
    lie,
As if some Protean art the change had wrought,
In listless quiet o'er the ethereal deep
Scattered, a Cyclades of various shapes
And all degrees of beauty.

The River Duddon, Sonnet, IV:

A Protean change seems wrought while I pursue
The curves, a loosely scattered chain doth make;
Or rather thou appear'st a glistering snake,
Silent, and to the gazer's eye untrue.

Hazlitt in his essay, *Character of Burke,*
complains that he can describe other orators,
but as for Burke, "Who can bind Proteus or
confine the roving flight of genius? "

Emerson abounds with references to Proteus; these three quotations will illustrate the
meaning that word bore in his writings.

Essay on History: "Each new law and

[89]

political movement has meaning for you. Stand before each of its tablets and say, ' Under this mask did my Proteus nature hide itself,' " and again in this same *Essay:* " The philosophical perception of identity through endless mutations of form makes him (man) know the Proteus. What else am I who laughed or wept yesterday, who slept last night a corpse, and this morning stood and ran? And what see I on any side but the transmigrations of Proteus? "

Essay on Nature: " The fable of Proteus has a cordial truth. Each particle (in nature) is a microcosm, and faithfully renders the likeness of the world."

Roden Noel: *Essays on Poets and Poetry,* page 264: In discussing Browning's great ability in psychological analysis and the difficulty there involved.

" The Protean soul ever eluding her own self-knowledge and the knowledge of others, by assuming infinite marks and shapes."

These quotations are only a selection from a vast number of references to Proteus in English literature.

His name has passed over into the realms of botany, biology, and zoölogy, denoting in each case extreme instability or changeableness. It has even entered the domain of slang, to denote an actor who is obliged to assume inferior and changing rôles.

References to this god are in all classes of literature, and a recent publication, *Jokes For All Occasions*, tries in the Introduction to give a definition of wit, then in despair adds: "It is as hard to settle a clear and definite notion of wit as it is to make a portrait of Proteus."

During the celebration of the festival of the Mardi Gras at New Orleans there is the Carnival or Ball of Proteus at which the leader assumes to be that divinity, and he must always appear in a new guise and a new costume. The ingenuity of uniform designers is taxed to make a new creation each year, a creation which must also show that the leader is assuming to be a divinity of the sea.

Proteus has even become a Christian name, and the full name of the great electrician is given as Charles Proteus Steinmetz. I do not know whether he had this name from birth or not, but the application of the name of the wizard of the sea to the wizard of electricity looks like an after-thought.

The widespread influence of this divinity is but typical of most of the creations of Homer. A Tantalus, Circe, or Niobe would show similar extension; while Helen, Hecuba, Hector, or Nestor would so overwhelm with material as to daunt the most eager student.

Even all these gods, heroes, fables, ideas, and words, so widely used and known, reveal but faintly the influence of Homer.

Aristotle founded his immensely important theory of poetry on what the *Iliad* and the *Odyssey* actually are, regarding them as the standard of perfection both in plan and in execution.

Professor Dixon says: " In the centuries during which the ideal of heroic poetry was in debate Homer was without a serious rival. He is without a rival still." [21]

His influence is to be estimated by the fact that at the very beginning of our literature he set up an ideal and gave an example which has inspired and guided all writers influenced by European civilization. He is the dominating force with those who have read him and also with those who have read him not, for he created the atmosphere in which liberalizing culture has continued to abide.

VIII. HOMER AMONG THE ANCIENT GREEKS

ALL Greek art, society, and literature assume the poetry of Homer as a background and a foundation. Xenophanes, the first writer in whose works is found the name of Homer, says: " From the beginning, for all have learned from him." Plato refers to him as the one who has trained Hellas, and calls him " the best and the most divine of poets," " the greatest of poets and the first of the dramatists."

He was regarded by entire Hellas as the greatest poet, the father of tragedy, the pattern for oratory, the source of theology, the leader in all civilizing pursuits, so that Plato called him: " the poet wise in all things."

Cicero could say with but little exaggeration: " Homer because of his outstanding excellence made the common name ' poet ' his own proper name," and Philo to the same effect: " Although there were unnumbered poets, Homer was meant when the word ' poet ' was used." [22]

Then by a sudden shift Homer was well-nigh deprived of his own name and Plato was called "*Homerus Philosophorum,*" Aesop, "*Homerus fabularum,*" Sophocles, "*Homericus Tragicus,*" and Sappho, "*the female Homer.*" In each case the word Homer was intended to convey superlative honor.

Coins were struck with his likeness, days were named for him, and recurring festivals celebrated in his memory. Artists strove to reproduce with paint, marble, clay, or metal his conceptions or his characters, and grammars were first needed and prepared in order to discuss the Homeric language.

Protagoras has the honor of being the first to discuss the significance of the moods, and his query regarding the use of the imperative in the first verse of the *Iliad,* whether or not a divinity should be addressed with an imperative, may well have been the first step towards a scientific treatment of that important part of syntax.

Homer used many words which were archaic even in his own age and which were difficult of interpretation in subsequent times, hence the need for explanation and the creation of lexica. The first of these were devoted solely to the elucidation of Homeric vocabulary. This fact was so familiar that poets of comedy could introduce parents questioning their children on the meaning of obsolete or obscure Homeric words.

The great Athenian dramas were regularly presented in Athens but a single time, yet the poetry of Homer and of Homer alone was recited at each recurring Panathenaic festival; thus it was kept constantly fresh in the public mind. The fact that the scholars of Alexandria used, in their recension of the text, copies from Sinope, Chios, Argos, and Marseilles, evidently state or public copies, shows that Athens could hardly have been alone in such recitals.

Greek audiences, despite the frequency with which they heard them, never wearied of listening to the Homeric poems, and an orator could be sure of arousing the interest of his hearers by repeating verses from the *Iliad* or the *Odyssey*.

Aeschines in a speech, supposed to have been delivered before a jury, paraphrased and quoted Homeric verses, then turned to the clerk and asked him to recite, first the passage where Achilles expresses his determination to avenge the death of Patroclus, then the words of the shade of Patroclus in which Achilles is begged to prepare a common burial place for them both, and next the warning of Thetis that the death of her son will follow close upon the slaying of Hector. The clerk is assumed to have recited at once the desired passages, twenty-six verses in all.

It seems most improbable that the clerk could have taken the time to search a manuscript in order to find the requested scenes, but he must have recited at once from memory. Aeschines never asked him if he knew the verses and seems to have taken that knowledge as a matter of course. Verses from Hesiod and Euripides are also quoted in this same speech, but Aeschines does not call upon the clerk to recite them, he does that himself.

This knowledge of Homer on the part of a clerk would be no novelty, since we know that Homer was committed to memory by the intellectual élite of the Socratic circle and we are told that even the Borysthenes almost all knew the *Iliad* by heart, although they were a rude people living on the banks of the distant Dnieper River.

Socrates in the speech given at his trial answered his advisers, who urged him to desist

from the search for truth and thus to follow
a safe course, by quoting the Homeric example
of Achilles, who preferred an early death to
seeming dishonor; then, when Socrates was con-
demned to death he consoled his friends and
himself with the hope that death would make
it possible for him to question Agamemnon and
Odysseus, and that he could be with Homer.
While he was in prison and his end was near
he thought a divine spirit had given him a
revelation through the medium of an Homeric
verse.

Wherever the Greeks went Homer went with
them. He was known from India to Marseilles,
from the Dnieper to the upper Nile, and so
great was his prominence that among the literary papyri found in Egypt about three hundred are from Homer, while the poet who ranks
as second in the number of such papyri is
Euripides, who has but twenty-seven.[23]

The career of Alexander the Great was
largely an attempt to realize the Homeric ideal
and to duplicate the glory of Achilles. Alexander on all his campaigns carried with him
a copy of the *Iliad*, calling it a perfect, port-
able treasure of military virtue. Many of that
conqueror's acts would have little meaning, if

we did not know that he was imitating both the passion and the extravagance of the Homeric hero.[24]

Homer was the greatest single force in making of the Greeks a kindred people and in giving them a mutually understandable language and common ideals. This poetry not only permeated all classes of society and reached the utmost confines of Greek civilization, but its influence continued throughout the entire Greek period itself, felt alike in Hesiod, the poet nearest in time to Homer, and in Julian the Apostate, who tried in vain to restore the ancient gods to a position of power and reverence. The last efforts made by Hypatia to bring back the beliefs and ideals of early Greece were connected with Homeric poetry.

The words of Dio Chrysostom: " Homer is first, middle, and last for every boy, for every man in vigor, and for every man in old age," hold true to all parts and to all periods of Greece, to a Plato and Aristotle in Athens and to shepherds and fishermen on the Pontus.

Heraclitus told the story of the glory that was Greece in these words: " Our earliest infancy was intrusted to the care of Homer, as if he had been a nurse, and while still in our swaddling clothes we were fed on his verses, as if they had been our mother's milk. As we grew to youth we spent that youth with him, together we spent our vigorous manhood, and even in old age we continued to find our joy in him. If we laid him aside we soon thirsted to take him up again. There is but one terminus for men and Homer, and that is the terminus of life itself." [This Heraclitus is not the famous philosopher but an interpreter of Homer living in the earlier years of the Roman Empire.]

Even the early Christians felt it necessary to connect their faith with the Homer of their fathers, hence they re-wrote the story of the birth, life, and death of Jesus into poems made up entirely of tags and of verses from Homer. We have such a poem, supposed to be the work of Patricius, a bishop, and of Eudocia, the empress and the wife of the younger Theodosius.

This poem is of such great significance as an illustration of the lasting reverence for Homer that I have thought it worth while to add here the translation of a part of it, the account of the birth of Jesus, the star and the shepherds. In these verses not a single change had been

made either in form or in arrangement of the
Homeric original.

But when the laboring goddess of childbirth, (Il.,
    XVI, 187)

One month just ending and another already begin-
    ning, (Od., XIV, 162)

Brought him to light, and he saw the rays of the
    sun, (Il., XVI, 188)

The year having finished its course, the hours came,
    (Od., XI, 295)

A gleam reached to heaven, and all the earth
    laughed. (Il., XIX, 362)

All the old men and likewise the young men also
    (Il., II, 789)

Were surprised and their spirit fell to their feet;
    (Il., XV, 280)

Then a star arose brightest of all, a star which
    (Od., XIII, 93)

Shines clearest, after it has bathed in the ocean,
    (Il., V, 6)

Showing a sign to men with its wonderfully bright
    beams, (Il., XIII, 244)

Which a shepherd in the fields with his flocks (Il.,
    V, 137)

Marveled at in his heart, for he believed it a god.
    (Od., I, 323).

Certainly these verses reveal but little of the account as given in the *New Testament,* but they do show a pathetic attempt to re-tell the story of Jesus in words with which these late Greeks and early Christians must have been thoroughly familiar, and they show also the long-continued influence of Homer.

With Homer Greek culture began, with him it flourished, with him it won dominion, with him it fell, and with him it rose again. He was the first adequately to express the Hellenic spirit and he was the last to keep it alive. No other great people has been so much the creation of a single person, and he was to the Greeks their law-giver, teacher, and poet, combining in himself the characters of Moses, David, and the prophets.

What the Greeks might have been, if there had been no Homer, we cannot guess, but what they were at their best was largely because of him. Hellenic influence is in no small measure the influence of Homer.

IX. HOMER AND ROMAN ITALY

THE Romans were slow in turning their minds to creative and imaginative literature, but long confined their efforts to short war songs, legal enactments, monumental inscriptions, annals, and short encomiums in praise of the dead or of ancestors. Homer was far from all these and exerted little or no influence on Roman thought until the end of the First Punic War, when Livius Andronicus created the first piece of literary work in the Latin language of which any important fragments have been preserved, and that was a version of the *Odyssey* composed in the native Saturnian verse.

Homer thus became in a measure for the Romans what he had been for the Greeks, the source of learning and letters, since this Latin *Odyssey* was the book used in the instruction of the young, and Horace as a boy, nearly two centuries later, was obliged to commit to memory from dictation this old Latin *Odyssey*.

The real beginnings of Latin literature date from the next generation with Ennius, known as the father of Latin poetry, who turned to the traditions of his own people for the theme of his epic, the *Annales*. Livius Andronicus had translated Homer into the Saturnian verse, but Ennius abandoned this native rhythm and in spite of the difficulties of the language wrote his epic in the dactylic hexameter of Homer, thus eliminating the native poetic tendencies.

Ennius believed that Homer had appeared to him in a vision and had assured him that his own soul had passed into the body of Ennius, hence his aspiration to be the Homer of Italy. The *Iliad* and the *Odyssey* furnished the poetic ideals and inspiration for the *Annales*. Skutsch, one of the best modern authorities, says: " Ennius showed that Homer's soul had possessed him, not only by the use of the Homeric hexameter and Homer's formulae, but also by the borrowing of phrases, verses, tags, and descriptions." [25] So thoroughly was the *Annales* permeated with the spirit of Homer that Ennius was called a second Homer, *alter Homerus*.

Cicero excused his own borrowings from Plato and Aristotle by saying that Ennius had transferred verses from Homer into his own poems.

Homer through Livius and Ennius became a dominating influence at the very beginning of Roman literature.

It is a striking indication of the immortality of Homer that, although he was older by many centuries than Ennius, his works have survived while the poetry of Ennius has practically disappeared, since we have but small fragments of his works, not over one-fortieth of the whole.

Ennius was native to the language of Greece, hence knew Homer in his own tongue and did not rely on the translation of the *Odyssey* which had been made by Livius. It was not until the end of the second century B.C. that the *Iliad* was translated into Latin, when Matius and Crassus each made a Latin version of the *Iliad*. Both used the hexameter of the original, as the Latin Saturnian had become obsolete; such was the preëminence of the Homeric meter.

With the beginning of the first century, the great age of Roman literature, the influence of Homer had become almost universal in Rome. Cicero tried his hand at translating into hexameters various passages from Homer, *e.g.*, the song of the Sirens and other famous passages. The longest continuous translation from Homer

which has been preserved in the works of
Cicero is the speech of Odysseus when he repeated to the Greeks the story of the nine
sparrows eaten by the serpent, giving a version
of thirty-two verses.

Cicero was an Homeric enthusiast and in
his *Pro Archia* he quotes the envious words of
Alexander, spoken at the tomb of Achilles:
" O fortunate Achilles who didst find in Homer
a herald of thy glory! " then Cicero adds:
" True indeed, for without Homer the same
mound that covers his ashes would cover his
glory also."

The letters of Cicero were written for pri-
vate purposes and not for publication or display, hence his quotations in them from Homer
prove that Homer was familiar to him and to
those who received the letters.

These Homeric quotations in the letters of
Cicero extend over the period from 65 to
44 B.C. In the letter to Atticus which is given
first place, *Ad Att.*, I, 1, 4, Cicero compares
the prize for which he is striving with that for
which Hector ran with Achilles in the race for
his own life, " Since he was not running to win
the hide of an ox or a sacrificial victim." In
the letter he wrote to Atticus in Nov. 44, he

put two quotations from Homer. Forty-nine of these letters have such quotations, some letters containing several. In a letter to Julius Caesar in which he recommends the son of a friend in his application for appointment to some official position there are four quotations from Homer, two of which have two entire verses, each. The tone of the letters shows that Caesar could be presumed to be very familiar with Homer, and this familiarity seems to have been common among the better Romans for several centuries. When Marcus Porcius Cato heard of the exploits of Scipio in Africa, he exclaimed: "He alone keeps his discretion, while all the rest as shadows flit about." (This is the description of Tiresias in the *Odyssey*.)

When he saw Carthage in flames, Scipio repeated the forebodings of Hector: "A day shall come when Troy shall fall, and Priam, and the people of Priam of good ashen spear," evidently foreseeing the fate of Rome in the ruin of Carthage. This same Scipio, when he heard of the death of the liberal and reformer, Tiberius Gracchus, exclaimed in the words of Athena concerning the doom of Aegisthus: "Thus may perish even another, whoever does such deeds." In Cicero's time of pride and glory Sextus quoted to him the words of Hector: "May I meet my end, not slothfully and ingloriously, but having finished some great exploit to be renowned even among future generations." [This was Sextus Peducaeus.]

As Brutus was about to sail from Italy his wife began to weep at sight of a painting which represented the parting of Hector and Andromache, when one of the friends repeated: "But Hector thou art to me father, mother, and brother, and thou art also my glorious husband." Brutus instantly took up the quotation and, smiling, said in the original Greek that unlike Andromache she was not bidden "to attend the loom and the distaff." This little incident with its setting shows how thoroughly at home Homer had become among the Romans. At a magnificent banquet in honor of his birthday, Brutus took up a cup, and, as he held it high, he pronounced the dying words of Patroclus: "An evil fate and Leto's son have brought me to ruin," — a verse which seemed prophetic of his own doom. When Brutus and Cassius were quarrelling, Marcus Favonius, a Roman senator, rushed into their presence and tried to calm them by quoting the speech of Nestor, beginning with the words: "Obey me, for you are both younger than I."

The Roman emperors in moments of excitement would quote Homer in his own language. It is said that Augustus, humiliated by the licentiousness of his daughter, repeated the words spoken to Paris by Hector: "O that you had perished unwed, or had ne'er been born." At another time, when Augustus made Tiberius his heir and successor, he quoted the words which Diomede had used regarding Odysseus, as he chose him his companion for a night foray: "If this man follows me, we can both come safely back even from blazing fire, since he is extremely shrewd in planning."

Even the brutal Caligula was so versed in Homer that he could shout to some subordinate kings who were striving among themselves: "Let there be one lord and one king," and he, Caligula, defied Jupiter with the words of Ajax: "Either raise me aloft, or I will raise you." Claudius reveled in his ability to quote Homer, and it is said that once when he punished a foe he ordered his death with the Homeric verse: "Ward off the man, since he has been the first to show violence." This foible of quoting verses from Homer is made the matter of clever satire by Seneca, who wrote a poem to glorify the emperor's admission to a place among the gods. When the officers of Nero had revolted and he was forced to flee, he knew that the horsemen were near who had been sent to capture him, and as he heard them approach he uttered the words of Nestor: "The sound of fleet steeds rings in my ears," and put his sword to his own throat.

The knowledge of Homer which these quotations indicate continued throughout all the period of the Empire and even survived its fall.

HOMER AND VIRGIL

HOWEVER, Homer's greatest influence on Roman letters and through them on subsequent centuries has been through none of the Caesars, but through the *Aeneid* of Virgil, a poem written under Homeric influence, abounding in Homeric scenes, and showing throughout Homeric imitation, and yet of such outstanding greatness that, although left unfinished, it has given its author a position that for centuries permitted him to challenge supremacy with Homer himself. Virgil is now given in

general a position subordinate to Homer, but
this is due to the rising estimate of Homer, not
to any less appreciation of Virgil.

The *Iliad* is a war poem, the *Odyssey* a
poem of travel and adventure, Virgil decided
to add a third poem to this small group, and
with the first words, *arma virumque cano,*
showed that he intended to cover the theme of
each of the other poems. The *Odyssey* told
of the wanderings and struggles of a victorious
Greek after he had left conquered Troy for
his home in the west, and the *Aeneid* shows the
other side of that picture by telling the fate of
the Trojans and the story of one of the conquered as he fled from that same Troy and also
sought a home in the remoter west. Each had
to win a victory and to conquer for himself a
place where he might live and rule.

The story of the *Aeneid* is thus exactly contemporary with that of the *Odyssey,* and
Aeneas must have been entertained at the court
of Dido at the very time that Odysseus was
lingering in the island of Calypso.

Virgil was obliged to depend on the *Iliad*
and the *Odyssey* for his descriptions of the
manners, implements, and customs of the civilization which formed the background for his

poem, since Homer was the only authority for the life of the heroic age.

The *Aeneid* was nothing less than the bold attempt to arouse Roman patriotism and to create national enthusiasm by means of a literary creation constructed on Homeric foundations and largely out of Homeric materials.

The *Iliad* furnished the hero, Aeneas the son of Venus and Anchises, and it also furnished the driving motive of the poem, the anger of Juno, and it likewise furnished the pattern for the war and the battles by which the native races were subdued. The *Odyssey* furnished the outline for the journeyings and for most of the adventures in or near fairyland, but the influence of both poems is evident in all parts of the poem, even if the first six books roughly correspond to the *Odyssey,* the last six books to the *Iliad.*

Some of the structural similarities with the *Odyssey* are the following: several years of the hero's wanderings have passed before the action of the poem begins; the hero is driven by a storm to a region where his glory is already known; Odysseus hears a song in which his own praise is sung and Aeneas sees representations of his own greatness done in bronze;

each is urged to tell of his wanderings and his name; and each takes up in the same manner the story of his miseries and adventures.

In both poems the story of the hero's own adventures is told in the first person, " I suffered this, or I did that," but when they leave the land to which they had been storm-driven, the poet tells the tale in his own person and both Odysseus and Aeneas act and speak in the third person.

The storm is similarly described in both, even the same minute details reappear, *e.g.*, Homer says: " Poseidon covered sea and land alike with clouds, and night came down from the heavens," and Virgil renders it thus:

Eripiunt subito nubes caelumque diemque
Teucrorum ex oculis; ponto nox incubat atra.

Aeneas as well as Odysseus passed by or near Scylla, Charybdis, Circe, and the Sirens, but it was obviously impossible for them both to have had similar adventures with the Cyclops, for that monster had but one eye, and this single eye could not have twice been blinded. Virgil introduced the shrewd device of having Odysseus abandon unknowingly one of his companions in the haunts of the Cyclops, then having this abandoned companion appeal to Aeneas for safety and tell to Trojan ears the horrible tale of the fate of his own associates within the cave of Polyphemus.

Jupiter sent Mercury to make known his purpose that Aeneas must not remain with Dido, as the same god was sent by him to Calypso to perform a like service concerning Odysseus.

Games were held in honor of Anchises, exactly as they had been held in honor of Patroclus. A ship-race is substituted for the chariot-race, but the incidents are very similar. In some of the other contests the very details of the *Iliad* are repeated. In the foot-race of the Homeric games Ajax, the son of Oileus, is about to win, when he slips and falls in the dung and filth of slaughtered oxen; so also Nisus who is in front of the runners falls down in the gore and filth of cattle which had just been slain.

In Homer's account of the contest in archery it is said that a dove was fastened by a thong to a pole or mast; then the announcement was made that the one who cut the thong would receive the second prize, the one who hit the bird would be the winner. In this contest

Teucer shot and missed the bird, but cut the thong so that the loosened bird flew aloft, but Meriones, who was all-prepared, slew the bird as it flew and thus won the first prize.

There is a logical difficulty in this contest, for had the first archer succeeded in the easier task of hitting the tethered bird the second archer could have had no contest, for he certainly would not have aimed at the thong. One would have supposed that Virgil could have made a slight change here and thus have provided a real contest, but he did not; for in this same contest in archery Mnestheus' shot severs the cord which bound the bird and as it flies aloft it is transfixed by the arrow shot from the bow of Eurytion. Virgil could not represent the great archer of the Trojans, Pandarus, as victor, for Pandarus had been slain, but he represents Eurytion as the brother of that treacherous bowman.

Such athletic contests as are described by both of these poets were the very life of the ancient Greeks and their greatest glory was the athletic prize, but such contests held no high place among the Romans, and the feelings aroused in a Greek by such descriptions had no counterpart in their emotions. The games in

[114]

Virgil are not only an imitation, but they are exotic, foreign to Latin life and thought.

Aeneas, too, was forced to take a trip to Hades in order to consult the shade of Anchises, just as Odysseus had made the same journey to consult the shade of Tiresias. When Odysseus was starting on this journey, one of his companions had died from accident unobserved by his companions; this shade of the unburied sailor met Odysseus before he entered Hades and begged him to perform the fitting burial rites, then erect on the top of his mound an upright oar, the oar with which in life he had rowed with his companions. Aeneas in a similar manner learns of the death of his follower and promises to erect for him a mound and on that mound to fix the oar with which he, Misenus, had rowed.

Aeneas as well as Odysseus found that a sword could not avail against the shades, for they were unsubstantial phantoms. The silent anger with which Ajax turned away from Odysseus furnished Virgil the chosen method for describing the meeting in Hades of Dido and Aeneas.

The description of the war which occupies much of the last six books of the *Aeneid*

abounds with incidents taken from the *Iliad;*
some of which are inevitable in Homer, but
have little motive in Virgil; Achilles had loaned
his own armor to Patroclus and he in turn had
lost it to Hector, so that Achilles was unpro-
tected and his mother then went to Hephaestus
to supply her son's need; the mother of Aeneas
makes the same trip to the same god and brings
divine armor for his protection. This armor
was an ornament, a means of display for
Aeneas, but it was a necessity for Achilles.

The walls defending the enemy were stormed
according to the Homeric methods of warfare,
and Aeneas' friend, Pallas, was slain; his death
was mourned with almost the same words by
which Achilles voiced his grief for Patroclus.
Aeneas in his anger also took alive sons of the
foe, to offer them as a propitiation for the
death of his friend. Aeneas and Turnus, like
Paris and Menelaus, agree to fight a duel which
shall decide the issues of the war and to see to
whom the hand of the princess shall be given,
but peace does not follow since Aeneas like
Menelaus was shot from secret ambush.

At last, when after many delays Aeneas and
Turnus meet for the decisive struggle, Jove
puts the destiny of each in the fateful scales,

when Turnus like Hector turns and flees while Aeneas follows in close pursuit; the poet, quoting Homer, says:

> neque enim levia aut ludicra petuntur Praemia, sed Turni de vita et sanguine certant.

When Turnus falls beneath the blow of Aeneas, he like Hector begs that the victor in mercy give his body to his own people; Aeneas hesitates but when he sees that Turnus wears the spoils he had stripped from Pallas, his own friend, he gives way to his anger and plunges his sword into the body of his fallen and helpless foe, and the poem ends with the words:

Vitaque cum gemitu fugit indignata sub umbras,

like the words with which Homer describes the death of Patroclus. It is no mere chance that the *Aeneid* begins and closes with Homer.

We cannot judge what Virgil might otherwise have written, but the present *Aeneid* without the *Iliad* and the *Odyssey* would have been an impossibility.

Daniel Heinsius, the great Latinist of Leyden, wrote with some exaggeration: Ut mihi optima Homeri editio Virgilianum poema videatur.

Conington said: "The Aeneid invites comparison with the *Odyssey* in the whole external form, even in the very title, and contains an imitation or a translation from Homer on almost every page," and Nettleship in his revision of Conington's Virgil adds: "Vergil considered it as his first duty to construct his epic in words, manner, and arrangement on the model of the *Iliad* and the *Odyssey*." [26]

Virgil went to Homer as to an inexhaustible mine for plot, for incident, and for ornament. Out of this material he created a Roman epic full of the highest patriotism, worthy of the glories of the Caesars and the greatness of the Empire.

Even the meter was a foreign and adopted meter; and it was really the praise of Homer which Tennyson uttered in his famous apostrophe to Virgil:

> *Wielder of the stateliest measure*
> *ever moulded by the lips of man,*

since it was the Homeric hexameter which appears as such stately melody in the measure of Virgil.

Such was the genius of Virgil that in spite of his indebtedness to the *Iliad* and the *Odys-*

sey he has been assigned a place of honor by the side of Homer himself, and during a period of almost one-thousand years Homer's influence was saved to civilization through the poetry of Virgil. The Greek epics were long unread in Europe but the *Aeneid* never passed into oblivion.

From the beginning of the rule of Augustus Homer could hardly be called a foreign poet in Rome, as the young were taught to read and to quote him in his own language. Horace and Ovid quote or refer to him with a familiarity like that of Plato and Aristotle, and seem to regard him as their own. Quintilian advised that reading should begin with Homer and Virgil, and Pliny wrote: " Boys in the forum should begin their legal training with civil cases, just as in school they begin with Homer." The habit among the Roman boys of learning Homer in the original Greek was long continued, since Augustine bemoaned the difficulty he found as a boy in appreciating Homer because of the strangeness of a foreign language, and Ausonius wrote to his grandson urging the importance of studying Homer.

It is said of S. Fulgentius, bishop of Ruspe

in the sixth century, that he had committed all of Homer to memory; while a boy (date uncertain) who died in Ferrara at ten years of age was honored with this epitaph: *Legi pia carmina Homeri.*

The maturer pupils were given themes from Homer to work over into rhetorical exercises, and the speeches of the *Iliad* and the *Odyssey* were studied as oratorical models and classified according to style and matter. These poems were recited in public and at banquets in much the same manner as in earlier ages of Greece, and Juvenal pictures women as forming clubs or societies to discuss the relative merits of Homer and Virgil.

Homer was part of the training and part of the mature life of educated Romans for not less than five-hundred years. A knowledge of his poetry was assumed and it was not affectation to quote him in his own language, since there were few who could not understand him.

The fact that a people who had gained empire without creating a single piece of pure literature which they cared to preserve should take over a foreign poet from a conquered people, adopt his meter, and make his poetry the ideal and the foundation for their own is the highest possible tribute which any nation could pay to a great poet.

The influence exerted by Roman literature during the Middle Ages and in our own time is largely the influence of Homer, for he is hardly less the father of Latin than of Greek letters.

X. HOMER AND THE RENAISSANCE

WITH the collapse of the Roman empire the knowledge of Greek and consequently of Homer rapidly diminished in western Europe so that by the end of the seventh century he was unknown outside of surviving Hellenic civilizations, except as he was quoted by Latin writers or found in cramped translations from the Greek. A little epitome of the *Iliad* in less than eleven-hundred verses, *Ilias Latina,* furnished for many centuries the chief source of knowledge regarding the poetry of Homer. Scholars in Constantinople and in the Greek regions of southern Italy never lost their knowledge of the original Greek and it was from these sources that Homer was returned to northern Italy, thence to the rest of Europe.

Dante knew no Greek and based his great tribute to Homer

Quegli è Omero, poeta sovrano

on the impression the *Iliad* and the *Odyssey* had made on others. Homer is quoted by

him six times, and all of these passages are
to be found in the Latin version of Aristotle
or in Horace.[27]   Homer exerted his influence
on him chiefly through the fact that Dante
chose Virgil for his guide in that famous journey to the regions inhabited by the dead, and
thus selected the sixth book of the *Aeneid,* a
book which depended very largely on the
eleventh book of the *Odyssey.*

The return of Homer to European civilization dates from the year 1354, since in that
year Sigeros procured in Constantinople for
Petrarch a Greek manuscript of the Homeric
poems.   Petrarch wrote to the donor: " You
have sent me from the confines of Europe a
gift than which nothing could be more worthy
of the donor, more gratifying to the recipient,
or more noble in itself.   Some make presents
of gold and silver, others again of jewelry and
the goldsmith's work.   You have given me
Homer, and, what makes it the more precious,
Homer pure and undefiled in his own tongue.
Would, however, that the donor could have ac-
companied his own gift! for, alas! your Homer
has no voice for me, or rather I have no ears
for him! Yet the mere sight of him rejoices
me, and I often embrace him and sigh over

him, and tell him how I long to hear him speak." For several years Petrarch was unable to find anyone who could read Homer to him or to secure a translation in either Italian or Latin. Later he made the acquaintance of a Calabrian Greek who knew Latin as well as his own native speech, and this Leontius Pilatus translated into Latin some passages of Homer for Petrarch.

This specimen translation so pleased Petrarch and Boccaccio that they urged him to make a complete translation of the *Iliad* and the *Odyssey* into Latin prose. Pilatus was invited to Florence, where in the home of Boccaccio and at the expense of Petrarch he completed this arduous task.

The manuscripts of Pilatus were given to Petrarch and they are now preserved in the Bibliothèque Nationale. The marginal notes in Petrarch's own handwriting may be seen in these manuscripts and attest the zeal and enthusiasm aroused in that great scholar by the Homeric poetry. It is said that Petrarch died with a copy of Homer in his hands, and that copy may well have been these manuscripts on which he so lovingly labored.

Boccaccio was not a whit behind Petrarch

in his admiration for Homer and he made free use of this translation by Pilatus in his own writings on the genealogy of the gods and in his comments on the *Divina Commedia*.

The knowledge of Homer rapidly spread, so rapidly that Bevenuto da Imola who is supposed to have completed his commentary on the *Divina Commedia* in 1380 quoted or referred to Homer about seventy times.

The restoration of Homer to the life of Europe was the joint work of Boccaccio and Petrarch; thus it lay right at the heart of the Renaissance.

The eagerness to read Homer in his own language could be satisfied in very few because of the difficulty of securing old manuscripts and the great labor involved in making new copies.

The noble Florentine, Bernardo de' Nerli, was eager to promote the study of Greek and after much consultation decided to publish the complete works of Homer. He furnished the means by which Demetrius Chalkondyles was enabled to edit and publish the first printed edition of Homer in Florence in 1488.

Evidently there was a great demand for copies of Homer, a demand not easily satisfied, since Aldus Manutius printed an edition in Venice in 1504 and a second edition was published by this same Aldus in 1517, and even a third in 1524. Meanwhile a Florentine printer, Giunta, had published in 1519 the *Editio Juntina*, and in a few years there was printed in Rome the so-called *Editio Romana*.

From Italy copies of Homer were soon carried throughout Europe, but the demand was so great that the Italian copies did not suffice, and four editions appeared from the press in Strassburg between 1525 and 1550, while two appeared in Basel in 1535 and 1541. Greek studies were rather late in getting a firm footing in England and the first edition of Homer to be printed in London did not appear until 1591, or more than a century later than the first edition printed in Florence.

Various treatises on epic poetry appeared early in Italy and Vida, the Bishop of Alba, again asked the question mentioned by Juvenal: " Which is the greater poet, Virgil or Homer? " a question which was long the source of many publications, as well as animosities.

Homer and Virgil were alike regarded as furnishing the norm of epic poetry, not Homer alone, as had been done in the writings of

Aristotle and in the criticism of the age of Augustus.

The danger from the advancing Turks which threatened Europe in the sixteenth century inspired Tasso with the idea of creating a poem which like the *Iliad* should describe a victorious attack on Asia by the forces of Europe, and thus retell the story of the Crusades in the manner of Homer.

Before he set himself to this task he devoted his energies to the study and mastery of the Homeric poems and he wrote a series of discourses on poetry, especially heroic epic poetry.

The contemplated poem, *Jerusalem Liberated*, was composed in this enthusiasm for Homer. The poem begins with " I sing," also an appeal to the Muse, while the introduction sets forth the general theme in the Homeric manner. The third and fourth verses:

> *molto egli oprò col senno e con la mano*
> *molto soffrì nel glorioso acquisto*

are plainly in imitation of the third and fourth verses of the *Odyssey*, where each verse also begins with the Greek word for much or many.

A quarrel of the heroes forms a central theme. There is also a dream sent to a leader, an assembly, a review of the army, and the Christian leaders are pointed out from the walls of the beleaguered city, also a duel and a traitorous shot which breaks the truce. Thersites has his coarse and babbling counterpart, and there is a procession like that sent to appease the goddess Athena. Throughout there are constant allusions which could hardly be understood by those ignorant of the *Iliad* and the *Odyssey*.

One passage where he follows Homer is very illuminating and that is the one which describes the distance of the island Pharos from Egypt and the Nile. The *Odyssey* says that Pharos is so remote from Egypt that a good ship with a fair breeze must spend an entire day in making the voyage. At the time of Tasso and of the Crusades which he describes, it was known that Pharos almost joined with Egypt, yet Tasso chose to follow Homer rather than known geographical conditions. It is likely that the description in the *Odyssey* rests on ignorance of the position of that island and that no important change has since occurred.

Tasso took a leading part in the discussion of the relative merits of modern poets and of Homer, and in answer to the critics of Homer he said: " If among mortal men there is anything immortal, nothing can as surely be endowed with eternal life as the poetry of Homer. He is more secure from the attacks of criticism and censure than is the summit of Olympus from the assault of storm and winds."

Italy went into intellectual decline in the seventeenth century, and the great cultural revival of the eighteenth century, " Il Risorgimento," was largely associated with the zeal for Homer, and it is said that at that time scarcely an important man of letters in Italy was ignorant of Homer in his own original language. It was in this atmosphere that Winckelmann made his first sojourn in Italy. A leading place in contributions to the appreciation and interpretation of Homer has been held by Italian men of letters and scholars ever since the time of Petrarch.

France, Spain, Holland, Scandinavia, Russia, and Germany, as well as Switzerland and Austria, have been mightily influenced by Homer and many of them have played important parts in the great advancement of Homeric studies during the last three centuries, but any valuable discussion of the influence of Homer among these nations is impossible in a book of such limited dimensions. The work done by Finsler in his *Homer in der Neuzeit* ably covers much of the field.

XI. HOMER AND ENGLAND

THE knowledge of Homer came to England directly from Italy, but certain traditions connected with the story of Troy were known through Virgil, Dares, Dictys, and the epitome of the *Iliad*, *Ilias Latina*, made by the so-called Pindarus Thebanus.

Both the French and the English believed that they were descended from the Trojans, hence they relied on the version assumed to be given by Dares, a Trojan priest of Vulcan.

Chaucer could hardly have known Homer at first hand, but in his *House of Fame* he sees Homer standing on a pillar of honor:

> *Ful wonder hye on a pileer*
> *Of yren, he, the greete Omere.*

Trojan descendents could not look with favor on the poet who had sung the glories of the Greeks, hence the verses:

> *But yit I gan ful wel espie*
> *Betwix hem was a litel envye,*

Oon seyde, that Omere made lyes
Feynynge in his poetries
And was to Grekes favorable.

The sixteenth century was the beginning of genuine and direct Greek influence in England. More in his *Utopia* described such an enthusiasm for the study of that language that all men were forced to become Hellenists by a decree of the senate of Utopia.

During that century Greek became a part of the curriculum in the universities, texts of Greek authors were published in London; even the Court studied Aristotle, Plato, and the Greek orators and tragedians. About the middle of the century Thomas Watson attempted a translation of Homer in English hexameters, and a little later Arthur Hall published a translation of the first ten books of the *Iliad*.[27]

Chapman achieved such a measure of success by his translation that he made Homer almost an English classic, and from this time to the present a knowledge of the contents of both the *Iliad* and the *Odyssey* has been part of the training of all educated Englishmen.

At the same time that Chapman was busy with his translation, Spenser was at work on his *Faerie Queene,* a poem which is permeated with Homeric mythology.

Shakespeare's productivity coincided in time with the translation of Chapman, a translation with which the poet was familiar, as is shown by the introduction into the story of *Troïlus and Cressida* of the character of the common reviler, Thersites, since that figure is not found either in Chaucer or in the mediaeval romance. Added proof that Shakespeare was familiar with the story of the *Iliad* is found in the manner by which Achilles is called back into action, since Shakespeare follows the Homeric account that it was the death of Patroclus which made Achilles forego his anger, while in the other version he returned because of the exploits of Troïlus.

An outline of the tenth book of the *Iliad* is found in the words of Warwick:

Our scouts have found the adventure very easy,
That as Ulysses and stout Diomede
With sleight and manhood stole to Rhesus' tents
And brought from thence the Thracian fatal steeds.

Henry VI, Part III, ιν, 2.

It is in Milton that the real spirit of Homer found English utterance, and it was with

Homer that Milton felt lifelong companionship. In a poem written when he was but
eighteen, *At a Vacation Exercise in the College,* he wrote:

Then sing of secret things that came to pass
When beldam nature in her cradle was;
And last of kings and queens and heroes old,
Such as the wise Demodocus once told
In solemn songs at king Alcinous' feast,
While sad Ulysses' soul and all the rest
Are held, with his melodious harmony,
In willing chains and sweet captivity.

The words " sad Ulysses' soul " show keen observation and the genius of the poet.

Comus is an Homeric poem in plan and setting. Comus was the son of Circe and like his
mother carried the wand of the magician and
gave his guests a potion which changed them
into beasts. His attendants were the debased
forms of human beings thus changed.

Odysseus was able to escape from Circe because of an herb, moly, which Hermes gave to
him, and it was with just such an herb that the
Good Spirit was able to baffle the efforts of
Comus.

Comus offers the lady a glass which was
said to contain a drink so joy-inspiring that,

Not that Nepenthes which the wife of Thone
In Egypt gave to Jove-born Helena
Is of such power to stir up joy as this.

The Homeric word which designated evening, " time for unyoking the oxen," becomes in the *Comus:*

what time the laboured ox
In his loose traces from the furrow came.

The song sung to invite Sabrina to come and release the Lady from the enchanter's spell calls upon Oceanus, Neptune, Tethys, Nereus, Proteus, Leucothea, Thetis, and the Sirens; all of whom are Homeric divinities.

Finally the Lady is released from the toils of Comus in much the same manner as the companions of Odysseus were restored to human forms after they had been turned into swine by the drug of Circe.

Milton in the *Comus* borrowed much from Homer, but it is first in *Paradise Lost* that he really caught the Homeric spirit; there it is not a matter of imitation but of a kindred mind rising to kindred heights.

Dryden thought that no one had ever copied Homer with such success as Milton, but

" copied " seems hardly the right word, rather say, comprehended Homer.

No translation gives me the thrill of the original; Chapman and Pope rarely strike the Homeric note, but when I read such verses as:

Highly they raged
Against the Highest, and fierce with grasped arms
Clashed on their sounding shields the din of war,
Hurling defiance toward the vault of Heaven,

I have all the sensations of reading Homer, for we have in these verses the grand style and the lofty melody.

Milton in a preface to *Paradise Lost* said that in abandoning rhyme he was merely following Homer.

The first words of this poem are in direct imitation of the *Iliad;* then Milton picks up his story in the Homeric manner, for Homer asks: " Who was it joined these two to fight in strife? " then adds, " It was the son of Leto and of Zeus." Milton asks:

What cause moved our grand Parents, to fall off
From their Creator,
Who first seduced them to that foul revolt?

Then like Homer answers his own question:
The infernal Serpent; he it was whose guile, etc.

[136]

The last verse of the *Iliad* is the simple and quiet sentence:

Thus then they buried Hector the knight.

Milton with similarly calm verses ends *Paradise Lost:*

They, hand in hand, with wandering steps and slow,
Through Eden took their solitary way.

Homer describes the staff of the Cyclops thus: " As we gazed at his staff, we likened it to the mast of a broad merchantship, a ship with twenty oars, a ship which makes its way over the great sea, so tall and thick was it."

This suggested to Milton the description of the spear or staff of Satan:

His spear — to equal which the tallest pine
Hewn on Norwegian hills, to be the mast
Of some great ammiral, were but a wand,
He walked with, to support uneasy steps.

In the first book of the *Iliad* Homer tells how Zeus in anger hurled Hephaestus from Olympus: " He hurled me, having seized me by the foot, from the heavenly threshold, and I fell during the entire day, coming just at sunset to the isle of Lemnos, when life was almost gone." Milton in praising the architect who created buildings for Satan, says:

N*or was his name unheard or unadored*
I*n ancient Greece; and in Ausonian land*
M*en called him Mulciber; and how he fell*
F*rom Heaven they fabled, thrown by angry Jove*
S*heer o'er the crystal battlements: from morn*
T*o noon he fell, from noon to dewy eve,*
A *summer's day, and with the setting sun*
D*ropt from the zenith, like a falling star,*
O*n Lemnos, the Aegean isle.*

Although this is all founded on Homer, no one could call it " copying."

The great difference between Milton and Homer is that Milton had a theological purpose, to " justify the ways of God to men," hence his poetry is argumentative; he carries on a demonstration, while Homer simply tells a story.

In sublimity, melody, and thought it seems to me that Milton can well claim equality with Homer, but in joining simplicity to sublimity Homer is all alone. Then Homer had the power to individualize almost numberless characters; he sympathized with the humblest, yet created the most exalted. Milton must remain

the poet for the educated only, while Homer
can be understood and enjoyed by all classes
of people. Much of the interest we feel for
Paradise Lost is aroused by our interest in the
poet. Homer arouses that same interest and
still remains hidden.

The creations of Milton live only in his
poetry, while those of Homer have moved out
of the verses of the *Iliad* and the *Odyssey* and
have become part of our traditions and ourselves. Helen, Ajax, Nestor, and Hector are
now almost independent of Homer.

The greatness of Milton is not in the story
but in the language itself and no one, so far as
I know, has collected for children or adults
stories based on *Paradise Lost,* while there are
scores of books retelling the tales of the *Iliad*
and the *Odyssey,* and even the outcasts in
Poker Flat are pictured by Bret Harte as
getting cheer and inspiration from reading
Pope's *Iliad,* even if they called Achilles
" Asheels."

During the time of Milton a translation of
both the *Iliad* and the *Odyssey* was made by
John Ogilby, but it obtained no great renown.
A little later Thomas Hobbes, the famous phi-

losopher, scientist, and author, translated both poems in iambic pentameter with alternate rhyming couplets. The introductory verses show the manner:

O *goddess sing what woe the discontent*
Of Thetis' son brought to the Greeks: what souls
Of heroes down to Erebus it sent,
Leaving their bodies unto dogs and fowls.

" Discontent " hardly expresses Achilles' feelings of rage.

Hobbes' rendering of the great scene which pictures Apollo's angry descent from Olympus will show how poorly the translator caught Homer's spirit and style:

His prayer was granted by the deity:
Who with his silver bow and arrows keen
Descended from Olympus silently
In likeness of the sable night unseen.
His bow and quiver both behind him hang.
The arrows chink as often as he jogs.

Nothing could be worse than this last verse; yet such was the zeal of the public to become acquainted with Homer that three editions of this work were soon demanded.

This was the age of John Sheffield, Duke of Buckinghamshire, and his *Essay on Poetry;*

the sum of his conclusions is expressed in the famous verses:

> Read *Homer* once, and you can read no more,
> For all books else appear so mean, so poor,
> Verse will seem prose; but still persist to read,
> And *Homer* will be all the books you need.

Johnson wrote: " Dryden may properly be considered as the father of English criticism," and Sir Walter Scott ranked him in poetry " second only to Milton and Shakespeare." It is fortunate that Dryden exercised his powers both as a critic and a poet on the poetry of Homer. He wrote a critique of Homeric poetry, translated the first book of the *Iliad* as a preliminary to the whole, and his own original poetry teems with Homeric allusions and imitations.

In the Preface to his *Fables* he writes: " I have found by trial Homer a more pleasing task than Vergil. For the Grecian is more according to my genius than the Latin poet. Vergil warms you by degrees; Homer sets you on fire all at once, and never intermits his heat." In a Dedication to Lord Radcliffe he refers to the bitter criticisms passed on Homer by Julius Scaliger and makes the famous comparison: " He would turn down Homer, and abdicate him after the possession of three thousand years. Who would not sooner be that Homer than this Scaliger? "

His own translation of the *First Book of The Iliad* is excellent, and the comparison made by Tennyson of parts of Dryden's translation with that of Pope may apply to much of the whole: " What a difference between Pope's little poisonous barbs, and Dryden's strong invective! And how much more real poetic force there is in Dryden! Look at Pope:

He said, observent of the blue-eyed maid,
Then in the sheath return'd the shining blade.

Then at Dryden:

He said; with surly faith believ'd her word,
And in the sheath, reluctant, plung'd the sword,"

In the years following Dryden, the beginning of the eighteenth century, Greek became almost a social necessity in England, so that Voltaire could later say that " few cultured English of his day were unfamiliar with Greek," and a knowledge of Greek meant a knowledge of Homer. Such writers as Temple, Wotton, Swift, and Addison show how keen the interest of the public was in discussions of that poet.

The satire on Homeric criticism which Swift published in his *Gulliver's Travels* would have been lost on any but the most ardent Homeric enthusiasts.

There was danger at this time that literature would withdraw from observation of life and nature and depend solely on Homer, a course advised by Sheffield in his verse, " Homer will be all the books you need," and especially in the verses of the youthful Pope in his *Essay On Criticism:*

Be Homer's works your study and delight,
Read them by day, and meditate by night,
Thence form your judgments, thence your maxims
    bring,
And trace the Muses upward to their spring.

Pope, not only by his translation but in all his poems shows his great indebtedness to Homer, especially in his great success, *The Rape of the Lock,* where the high language of the *Iliad* is made to carry the most trivial theme. The adaptation of the disdainful oath of Achilles is superb:

But by this lock, this sacred lock, I swear
Which never more shall join its parted hair,
Which never more its honors shall renew,
Clipp'd from the lovely head where late it grew.

The furor raised by this poem testifies to the wide reading of the Homeric poems.

Few men have ever received the honors and the rewards in their own day by their own original creations that Pope won by his translation of Homer. It made him comparatively wealthy and absolutely famous.

The industrious epic poets of this age were Blackmore, Glover, and Wilkie, whose writings were far more in bulk than Homer's, as they contained almost 100,000 verses. These poets set for themselves the ideal of taking Homeric materials, the Homeric example, and then rivalling Homer. The reviewers of their poems compared them with Homer and noted success or failure as they approached or departed from this standard.

' English letters in the middle of the eighteenth century were saved from the morass of senseless imitation by the discovery of the poetic value of the old English ballads, especially those in Thomas Percy's *Reliques of Ancient English Poetry,* 1765, and the publication at the same time of the *Complete Works of Ossian.* Up to this time Homer had through the influence of the writings of Aristotle been the ideal of cultured poetry, and now by a

strange stroke of fate he was found to be the
representative of the ballad as well, and an
entirely new aspect was assumed by the studies
of the ballad and by the studies of Homer.

The bards of the ballads were supposed to
be kindred to the wandering bards who composed and recited the songs of Homer. Mac-
pherson asserted that the songs of Ossian were
not committed to writing, but were preserved
in the memory of many generations of bards;
a statement which gave birth to the theory
that Homeric poetry had originated without
writing and that it too had been long carried
solely in the memory of the bards or minstrels.

Homer was the ideal of English classicism,
yet the swing away from that classicism was
a swing towards Homer, and the first great
English poet after Pope, one of the poets to
lead the English writers back to simplicity,
Cowper, felt it necessary to translate Homer in
simpler, yet heroic verse. This translation at
that time by such a poet as Cowper shows that
the revulsion against the assumed followers of
Homer was no revulsion against the poet
himself.

It is a startling proof of the influence of
Homer in the seventeenth and eighteenth cen-

turies that Milton should have written the *Comus* and *Paradise Lost*, that Dryden should have completed in part a translation of the *Iliad*, and that both Pope and Cowper should have transferred the Homeric Poetry into English verse. It can be safely said that no other writer, not even Shakespeare, possessed anything approaching this influence in these centuries.

The nineteenth century saw few real attempts to produce epics after the manner of Homer and Virgil. That period was given over to romantic poetry, to metaphysical introspection, and to enthusiasm for science, rather than to the impersonal telling in a grand style of the story of the exploits of heroes. Byron said of his own *Don Juan:*

> *My poem is epic, and is meant to be*
> *After the style of Virgil and Homer,*
> *So that my name of epic is no misnomer.*
>
> Canto I, 200.

It is hard to imagine a poem whose plan less resembles the *Iliad* or the *Odyssey* than *Don Juan,* as there is no beginning, no middle, and no end, and the detachment from his work of the early epic poet is entirely lost.

[146]

Byron speaks of Southey's longer poems:

While Southey's epics cram the creaking shelves.

Southey himself in his introduction to *Modoc* refused to call that poem an epic.

The *Idyls of the King* are rather a grouping around a central theme than an ordered epic, while the lengthy poems of Morris are not poems of action and epic movement, and the two poems by Matthew Arnold, *Sohrab and Rustum,* and *Balder Dead,* although modeled on Homer, are rightly classed by the poet himself as " Narrative Poems " and not as epics.

Professor Dixon was not wrong when he said: " The nineteenth century in England made no attempt to comply with the requirements of formal epic." [28]

Wordsworth naturally showed little traces of Homeric influence, as his themes and his outlook were entirely foreign to the early classic epic, but in his Introduction to the *Ode to Lycoris* he tells of his early love for Homer and how he never wearied of going over the Homeric scenes; also, he wrote this critical judgment on a blank leaf of Ossian:

Such was blind Maeonides of ampler cast.

[147]

Shelley was an Homeric enthusiast, and we know from his own diary that he read all of Homer in the winter of 1814–15, and that he was working on the poetry of Homer in the year 1817. He refers to Homer as " King of Melody." And the beautiful chorus in which he voices the hope of a restored Hellas is Homeric:

> A *new Ulysses leaves once more*
> *Calypso for his native shore.*

Keats wrote his sonnet *On First Looking Into Chapman's Homer,* also a sonnet *To Homer,* and took the Homeric description of the Titans for the main conception of the situations of the first and second books of *Hyperion,* while Homeric mythology and illustrations permeate his poetry. Elton says: " Keats moved away from Spenser towards Homer and got the grand style." [29]

The favorite poet of the Victorian Age was Tennyson and his poetry is the voice of much of that great period.[30] He is said to have regularly taken with him on his travels a copy of Homer, to have translated aloud the *Odyssey* to Mrs. Tennyson, and his last rational

conversation was regarding Homer, as Doctor
Walter Leaf himself with whom the conversation was held, has told me.

This life-long affection for Homer is shown
by his poetry. He speaks of his English Idyls
as " faint Homeric echoes, nothing-worth."
Oenone, an epic fragment with the setting and
colors of the *Iliad, The Lotos-Eaters,* suggested
by the story of the *Odyssey,* and the *Choric
Song,* all read like Homer. In *A Dream of
Fair Women* Helen appears and speaks as in
the old epics. The home of the glorified
knights is described exactly as Olympus is
pictured in the *Odyssey:*

> *Where falls not hail or any snow,*
> *Nor ever wind blows loudly.*

It was his *Ulysses* that brought him into the
favor of the government and the poem which
seemed especially to give him the feeling of
great accomplishment. He tried his hand at
putting parts of the *Iliad* into English verse,
wrote a short poem in alternate hexameters
and pentameters, *On Translations of Homer,*
and in 1888 wrote another poem, *To Ulysses,*
which begins with the verse:

> *Ulysses, much-experienced man,*

words suggested by the first verse of the *Odyssey*.

Near the end of his life he wrote *Parnassus,* closing with the optimistic verses:

If the lips were touch'd with fire from off
a pure Pierian altar,
Tho' their music here be mortal need the
singer greatly care?
Other songs for other worlds! the fire
within him would not falter;
Let the golden Iliad vanish, Homer here is
Homer there.

Not even Shakespeare so profoundly influenced the genius of Tennyson as did the poetry of Homer.

The great critic of that same age was Matthew Arnold, who added to the sanity of a critic the genius of the poet. Arnold's most famous critical work is a series of essays *On Translating Homer.* In these essays he assigns to Homer the first rank and says that Homer always composes at a level only reached by Shakespeare, when Shakespeare is at his best. *Sohrab and Rustum* is a Persian tale with Homeric incidents told in Homeric language, while *Balder Dead* is largely a trans-

[150]

ference of Homeric speeches and plot to a
Scandinavian legend. Such verses as these, to
one who has like Ulysses come to the realm of
the dead,

> Unhappy, how hast thou endured to leave
> The light, and journey to the cheerless land
> Where idly flit about the feeble shades?

are boldly taken from the mouth of Anticlia,
Ulysses' mother, and it seems startling to hear
Balder quote a speech of Achilles:

> Gild me not my death!
> Better to live a serf, a captured man,
> Who scatters rushes in a master's hall,
> Than be a crown'd king here, and rule the dead.

Homer is hardly less prominent in the thought
of Arnold than he was in that of Aristotle, despite all the accomplishments of the interven-
ing centuries.

Ruskin was no less under the spell of Homer
than was Arnold and he saw in him the ideal,
the standard of literary excellence. Few parts
of Homer were neglected by him, as I have
found that he has quoted in his writings every
book of the *Iliad* but one, and all the books of

[151]

the *Odyssey* but three, or that he has quoted forty-four books in all. Some of these books are quoted many times, so that the quotations from Homer number several hundred, while the allusions are almost numberless, and they are found alike in his earliest and his latest works.

In the mind of Ruskin Homer and culture are almost identical terms: " All Greek gentlemen were educated by Homer, all Roman gentlemen by Greek Literature, all Italian, French, and English gentlemen by Roman Literature and its principles. It does not matter how much or how little one may have read of Homer everything has been moulded by him."

This universal indebtedness to Homer might seem to fail in the modern novel, but Emerson wrote in the same strain as Ruskin: " Every novel is debtor to Homer," and Emerson also wrote the verses:

That wit and joy might have a tongue
And earth grow civil Homer sung.

Andrew Lang, the essayist, anthropologist, poet, and critic, wrote much in praise and in interpretation of Homer and collaborated in the famous prose translation of both the *Iliad* and the *Odyssey*. He used these striking words: "In the front of all poetry stands the poetry of Hellas, and in its foremost rank stands the epic of Homer. If we were offered the unhappy choice whether we should lose Homer and keep the rest of Greek poetry, or keep the rest and lose Homer, there could be little doubt as to our choice. We would rescue the *Iliad* and the *Odyssey*." [31]

That remarkable sentence was written by a man who appreciated Sappho, Pindar, Aeschylus, Sophocles, and the illustrious rest, and who knew literature as few men of any age have known it.

Stephen Phillips founded his *Marpessa* on the story told by Phoenix in the ninth book of the *Iliad,* and his *Ulysses* is a dramatic version of the *Odyssey*. His great scene between Ulysses and Calypso retells a like scene found in the fifth book of the ancient poem, while all the scenes in the palace of the hero and in Ithaca are based on the Homeric original.

Phillips caught the Homeric spirit, and the verse in which Penelope describes to her absent husband, to whom she appeals in her imagination, the maturity of Telemachus:

Thy son is tall, thou wilt be glad of him

[153]

shows the keenest comprehension of Greek
feeling and Homeric simplicity.

Ulysses in Homer yearned rather for his
kingdom and lost power than for his wife, but
Phillips, following modern sentiment, made
love for the wife the compelling passion, but,
even so, there are few poets in any age who
have been better interpreters of that great epic.

A little book by Arthur Machen, *Hiero-
glyphics,* tries to fix a standard by which really
great literature is to be judged and reaches the
conclusion that all such literature is to be
tested by the measure of its resemblance to
Homer. For this standard he selects the
Odyssey but is unable to tell in what the excellence of that poem consists or to give the
reasons for his choice: " We have only to bow
down before the great music of the *Odyssey,*
recognizing that by the very reason of its tran-
scendent beauty, by the very fact that it tres-
passes far beyond the world of our daily lives,
beyond selection and reflection, it is also exalted above our understanding, that because
its beauty is supreme, therefore its beauty is
largely beyond criticism. For ourselves we
do not need to prove its transcendence of life
by this or that extraordinary incident; it is

the whole spirit and essence and sound and
colour of the song that affect us; and we
know that the *Odyssey* surpassed the bounds
of its own age and its own land just as much
as it surpasses those of our time and own
country."

Appreciation of Homer in England never became professional and academic, even if the
universities have taken an illustrious part in
Homeric studies, but it has been shared by
cultured men in all walks of life. Chapman,
Milton, Dryden, Addison, Swift, Pope, Cowper, Tennyson, Arnold, Ruskin, Symonds,
Lang, Stephen Phillips, Samuel Butler, Arthur
S. Way, William Morris, and Mackail were
poets or men of letters; Hobbes, who translated Homer, was a philosopher; Edmund
Burke, who drew largely on Homer for the
arguments and illustrations used in his *Philosophical Enquiry into the Origin of the Sub-
lime and the Beautiful,* was philosopher, orator,
and statesman; Robert Wood, whose travels
and investigation of Homeric lands opened up
a new field of studies, was a statesman and
traveler. Robert Wood tells the following incident concerning Lord Granville, which shows

[155]

how familiar that statesman was with Homer and what familiarity could be expected in others: " Being directed to wait upon his lordship with the preliminary articles of the Treaty of Paris, I found him so languid, that I proposed postponing my business, but his lordship insisted that neglect of duty could not prolong his life and repeated with calm and determined resignation seven verses in the original of the speech of Sarpedon." These seven verses are thus translated by the Earl of Derby:

O *friend! if we, survivors of this war,*
Could live, from age and death for ever free,
Thou shouldst not see me foremost in the fight,
Nor would I urge thee to the glorious field:
But since on man ten thousand forms of death
Attend, which none may 'scape, then on, that we
May glory on others gain, or they on us.

It is hardly less remarkable that this aged statesman should have uttered these words of Homer than that this subordinate should have instantly caught their meaning and their purpose.[32]

Colonel William Mure of Caldwell, the great champion of a single Homer and brilliant

Homeric scholar, was for many years a member of Parliament.

The Earl of Derby, three times prime minister, translated the entire *Iliad* into the heroic verse of Milton; a translation which is regarded by many as the best in our language.

Gladstone, four times prime minister, was a constant producer of books and pamphlets on Homer, and he has the great distinction of being the first to turn public attention to the importance of the excavations made by Schliemann, and Schliemann reciprocated by dedicating to him the book which told of the astounding discoveries made at Mycenae.

Grote, the banker, started a new epoch in theories of Homeric composition by his work on the origin of the *Iliad;* and two of the outstanding Homeric scholars of our own day are Walter Leaf, a leading banker, and Alexander Shewan, formerly of the East India service.

Payne Knight, editor of a famous edition of Homer, was a wealthy art-connoisseur and a dilettante; Henry Dunbar, compiler of a *Concordance to the Odyssey*, was a distinguished physician; Austin Smyth, author of a book on the composition of the *Iliad*, is librarian of the

House of Commons; and H. B. Cotterill is a critic and historian of art, while a long line of clergymen or men who have received holy orders, extending from Bentley to Collins, became illustrious by reason of contributions to the appreciation of Homer.

The influence of Homeric poetry in England has been both broad and deep, hardly less felt there than in ancient Greece and Italy.

XII. HOMER AND
HIS PERMANENT INFLUENCE

HOMER is now only partially represented by the pages of the *Iliad* and
the *Odyssey*, for if these poems could
somehow be erased from the minds and traditions of men, his influence would be lessened
but not destroyed. The *Iliad* and the *Odyssey*
are like a great investment which has been ac-
cumulating interest, compound interest, for
nearly two thousand years.

He is the man with the five talents who has
gone out and made with them other five talents,
and he has been thus occupied for many centuries, so that Homer now represents not only
the principal but also the accrued interest. He
has drawn interest for only about two thousand years, since his talents were hid in darkness if not in a napkin for about a millennium,
that is during the centuries before the revival
of learning.

The accomplishments in epic poetry have all
been due to him, and no European poet unin-

fluenced by Homer has ever succeeded in the epic sphere.

Elegiac poetry began with the Homeric dialect, with the Homeric meter slightly modified, and flourished in Homeric soil. The early elegiac poets practically confined their vocabulary to words which had already been used by Homer.

Homer was called the first of the dramatists. Aeschylus said in pride and not in humility that his plays were courses from the Homeric feast, and the Athenian drama was so thoroughly under the spell of Homer that a Victor Hugo could write: " All the ancient authors of tragedy retail Homer, — the same fables, the same catastrophes, the same heroes. All draw their waters from the Homeric rivers. It is everlastingly the *Iliad* and the *Odyssey* over again."

Literary criticism became scientific in Aristotle's *Poetics* which was based on the *Iliad* and the *Odyssey* as standards, while Horace, Longinus, Sidney, and Saintsbury have followed in his steps. Pope cleverly says that Aristotle in his literary theories was guided by the Maeonian star.

Herodotus and the Greeks generally looked

[160]

upon Homer as the creator of history and one of those who had given to Hellas a definite and workable mythology and theology.

Homer was also considered as the discoverer of the true principles which regulate effective public speaking; Quintilian in his great work, written almost one thousand years after Homer, said of him: " Homer not only gave birth to but has furnished an example of every distinguished sort of oratory. No one has ever surpassed him in treating great matters sublimely or small things fittingly. He is both diffuse and contracted, delightful and dignified, wonderful alike by his abundance and his brevity, most eminent not only in the greatness of a poet but also in the greatness of an orator."

He was regarded as the father of philosophical and ethical doctrines not only by his own people but by the Romans as well. Horace wrote to his friend Lollius: " While you are reciting Homer at Rome I have re-read him at Praeneste. He tells us better than the philosophers Chrysippus and Crantor, what is honorable or disgraceful, what is useful or vain." Then Horace points out how certain moral qualities are made vital in the lives of Nestor, Ulysses, Paris, and other Homeric actors.

Physicians have seen in the accuracy with which wounds, their results and their treatment have been described, a sure indication that the poet himself was a physician, while military leaders have read these same poems and been convinced that he was a tactician.

Homer's sympathetic and exact portrayal of so many forms of vegetable and animal life shows that he was a most careful observer, even if he was not a trained naturalist, while his descriptions of gardens, armor, and especially of the shield of Achilles prove that he had the heart and the eye of the artist.

Homer is coequal with all classes of men; as he is contemporary with all ages, he does not grow out of date. We feel that Chapman, Pope, and Cowper belong to times that are no more, while Homer is young, fresh, and of our own day.

The greatness of Homer consists in this that he saw things and people exactly as they are and he could describe all these in such clear and simple language that we can see them too. This is the reason that a child can comprehend him, and that the wisest man knows that the greatness of Homer, with its simplicity, lies just beyond his grasp.

Sir Walter Scott read with enthusiasm Pope's *Homer* before he was of school age, and Browning at five was thrilled by the story of the *Iliad* which his father made realistic for him. Schliemann when a poor outcast boy at work in poverty and misery heard the sounds of hope in the music of Homer and saw a great vision. Schliemann's career of almost fabulous achievements was due to the persistence with which he followed that Homeric vision.

It is a long reach from the boyhood of these three to the maturity of an Aristotle, a Milton, and a Tennyson, but the one group seems hardly nearer to Homer than the other.

It is easy to gauge the mental stature of one who enjoys Milton, Emerson, or Browning by the very fact of that enjoyment, but the appreciation of Homer is conditioned by no mental or educational tests, for he adapts himself to all who read him and to all who hear him.

When Homer says of the laughter of the angry Hera, " She laughed with her lips, but there was no joy in her face," or when he said of the cup given by grudging charity, " It moistens the lip but it does not reach to the palate," or when he tells of the captive women who joined Briseis in her lamentations, " They

[163]

wept, seemingly for Patroclus, but each was thinking only of her own sorrow," he goes so much deeper and says so much more than the few words seem to imply.

The ability to clothe great ideas in simple language and to put the weightiest permanent truths into noble and lucid form gives a sufficient guarantee for the continued influence of Homer.

NOTES AND BIBLIOGRAPHY

ALL translations are by the author, unless the source is named.

NOTES AND BIBLIOGRAPHY

1. Leaf, Walter, "The Manuscripts of the Iliad," in *The Journal of Philology*, XVIII, (1890), 180–210.

2. Julian, 347 C.

3. This Inscription is published in Oxford Homer, V, 243.

4. Schmidt, Nathaniel, "Bellerophon's Tablet and the Homeric Question in the Light of Oriental Research," in *Transactions and Proceedings*, Am. Phil. Association, LI, (1920), 56–70. Professor Schmidt sees in the folded clay-tablets of Babylon the explanation of the secret message carried to Lycia.

5. Shepard, W. P., "Chansons de Geste and the Homeric Problem," in *American Journal of Philology*, XLII, (1921), 193–233. This article has never attracted the attention it so richly deserves. The many parallels are most illuminating.

6. Scott, John A., *The Unity of Homer*. Berkeley, California, 1921. In this the discussion of the origin of the Homeric poems is given at length, and it also contains a somewhat extended bibliography of that subject. Hence the omission of both discussion and bibliography in this book.

7. Wirth, Hermann, *Homer und Babylon*, pp. 19 ff. Freiburg, 1921.

8. Leaf, Walter, *Troy, A Study in Homeric Geography*, London, 1912, contains an extended and most valuable discussion of the historical setting of the *Iliad*. His *Homer and History*, London, 1915, takes up the history and geography of the Greek "Catalogue of Ships" and of the *Odyssey*.

9. Robert, Carl, *Bild und Lied, Archaeologische Beiträge zur Geschichte der griechischen Heldensage*, 95 ff.

Volume V of the *Philologische Untersuchungen* edited by A. Kiessling and U. von Wilamowitz-Moellendorff.

10. Bréal, M., *Pour Mieux Connaitre Homère*, p. 104. Paris, no date.

11. Keller, Helen Adams, *The Story of My Life*, p. 110. New York, 1902.

12. Lubbock, Sir John, *Introduction* to Pope's *Iliad*. London, 1891. Sir John quotes Pope's translation of *Iliad* VI, 263, to prove that Hector regarded Paris as the husband of Helen and not her paramour. "*But thou thy husband rouse and let him speed.*" The real translation is, "*But send thou this man on.*" The word husband is not suggested by the original.

13. Coleridge, S. T., *Biographia Literaria*, II, 11.

14. *The Goblet of Life*, ninth stanza.

15. Napoleon while encamped on the plains of Lombardy is said to have brooded over the fate of Achilles. Symonds, J. A., *Studies of the Greek Lyric Poets*, I, 123.

16. The figures for similes and tropes are given by Rothe, Karl, in *Die Odyssee als Dichtung*, p. 266. Paderborn, 1914.

17. Dixon, W. M., *English Epic and Heroic Poetry*, p. 20. London, 1912.

18. Sheppard, J. T., *The Pattern of the Iliad*. London, 1922.

19. Evans, Sir Arthur, *Palace of Minos at Knossos*, p. 698. London, 1921.

20. Spiess, Heinrich, *Menschenart und Heldentum in Homers Ilias*. Paderborn, 1913.

21. Dixon, page 24 of work just quoted.

22. On Homer as the "poet," Professor A. M. Harmon in *Classical Philology*, XVIII, (1923), pp. 35 ff. and a paper by me in *The Classical Journal*, XVII, (1922), pp. 330 ff.

23. These figures are those of Sir Frederic Kenyon as published in *The Journal of Hellenic Studies*, XXXIX, (1919), pp. 1 ff. Since the publishing of his figures important Homeric papyri have been discovered and published by professors of the University of Michigan.

24. Symonds, J. A., *Studies in the Greek Poets*, Chapter

on Alexander, suggested to me this paragraph on Achilles and Alexander.

25. The article on " Ennius " in Pauly-Wissowa.

26. Conington, John, *Introduction to the Aeneid.* London, 1872–6.

27. This chapter on the Renaissance is heavily indebted to Finsler, Georg, *Homer in der Neuzeit von Dante bis Goethe,* Leipzig und Berlin, 1912; also to a paper by Professor Cornelia G. Coulter, not yet published; and to Toynbee, Paget, *Dante Studies and Researches.* London, 1902.

28. Dixon, the work already quoted, p. 278.

29. Elton, Oliver, *A Survey of English Literature from 1830–1880.* London, 1912.

30. Mustard, W. P., *Classical Echoes in Tennyson.* New York, 1904. This little book is a remarkable combination of erudition and literary appreciation.

31. Lang, Andrew, *Homer and the Epic,* p. 3. London, 1893.

32. Wood, Robert, *The Original Genius of Homer,* Page VII. London, 1769.

Several books to which I have not referred in the above list have been much used by me.

ALLEN, T. W., *Homer, The Origins and the Transmission.* Oxford, 1924.

DRERUP, ENGELBERT, *Homerische Poetik,* Vol. I. Wuerzburg, 1921.

LUDWICH, ARTHUR, *Aristarchs homerische Textkritik.* Leipzig, 1884–5.

MACKAIL, J. W., *Virgil,* in the Series " Our Debt to Greece and Rome." Boston, 1922.

STUERMER, FRANZ, *Homerische Poetik,* Vol. III. Wuerzburg, 1921.

TOLKIEHN, J., " de Homeri auctoritate in Romanorum vita," in *Jahrbb. f. c. Phil. Suppl.,* XXIII, 222–289 (1897).

TOLKIEHN, J., *Homer und die roemische Poesie.* Leipzig, 1900.

Our Debt to Greece and Rome

AUTHORS AND TITLES

AUTHORS AND TITLES